CW00418777

BECOME A WRITER

A STEP-BY-STEP GUIDE

By

ANN EVANS

BECOME A WRITER
A STEP-BY-STEP GUIDE

With grateful thanks to Rob Tysall - Pro Photography
for the cover design.

Published by
Words & Images UK

ISBN: 9781652910985

Dedicated to everyone who has ever attended any of my writing workshops or courses.
Good luck with your writing ambitions – and remember, perseverance is the key.

Contents

Introduction

Becoming a writer is a dream for so many people. And why not? Writing is a wonderful, creative outlet. It's therapeutic, it's absorbing, it can be exciting and fulfilling. You can make a career from writing or you can write purely for fun and relaxation.

For me, it started more than 30 years ago as a hobby while bringing up three small children and helping my husband run a car respraying business from home. Somehow, writing turned into a passion, a full-time career, and a way of life.

I discovered that writing is like any other craft, we learn through study, we learn from others, and we learn by practice. You don't need to be 'born a writer', in fact, I wonder if anyone ever was. Most of the successful writers I know or have read about, have learned their craft through hard work and perseverance.

What I've also discovered over the last 30 years, is that we learn by experience, through making mistakes then (eventually) rectifying them and moving forward. So often, as we're just starting out on our writing journey, we don't know we're making mistakes. It's only when it's pointed out to us that we can put it right. Over the years I'm so grateful to the editors and other writers who took the trouble to point out the errors I was making in my writing.

My own writing journey has resulted so far in almost 40 books published, around 2,000 magazine and newspaper articles published on almost every topic under the sun. Add to this a few book, short story and article awards under my belt and I feel suitably qualified to help other writers to achieve their ambitions.

I love to see other writers doing well, so if passing on my knowledge and life's experiences to other budding writers is of help, then I'm only too pleased to do so.

I don't have all the answers, but I can point you in the right direction, and highlight the right and wrong ways to go about this amazing writing journey so many of us have embarked upon.

So, here it is, 30 years' experience wrapped up in a couple of hundred pages. I hope it's of use to you, and I hope you enjoy it.

Happy writing, everyone…

Ann Evans

Chapter One:
Make Time to Write

Step 1: Getting Organised

Many people fail in their writing ambitions simply because they can't get organised and make the time to write. People lead such busy lives that they might feel guilty about sitting down to write. There are so many other things demanding their time: family life, work, housework, shopping, gardening, cooking, DIY, socialising, holidaying, watching TV, social media and so on.

Of course, all these things are important and necessary but if you wait until you've dealt with all the usual chores and activities before you give yourself permission to indulge in your passion for writing, you will never start. So, don't let writing be bottom of your list of priorities.

Just as you allot time for your work, family life and social life, allocate some specific time *every day* to write, even if it's only half an hour or less; even if it's just a description of something you see around you. It doesn't matter what you write, just so long as you write.

Writing regularly will improve your skills and help you to feel like a writer. Plus, it shows others around you how committed you are and so they will hopefully respect your ambitions. Although I say that slightly 'tongue in cheek'.

Thinking back to when my three children were small, I would have my typewriter, papers and 'how-to' books scattered around the living room table. (How that table wobbled and rattled as my fingers tippy-tapped away.)

I'd perhaps get five minutes at a time without an interruption, in between breaking up squabbles over toys, changing nappies or running down the garden to husband's workshops to mask up a windscreen or polish a wheel trim. At mealtimes, the typewriter and papers would be pushed to the middle of the table, so we ate around the clutter.

Looking back, that period of my writing life bore a similar resemblance to working in the Features Department of the *Coventry Telegraph* some years later. But more on that later. The point is, no matter how busy you are, make time for your writing.

Make time for yourself

Set yourself a specific time which is your *writing time* and stick to it. If you're thinking there aren't enough hours in the day as it is, then make time. Try getting up an hour earlier or go to bed an hour later. Allocate this time specifically for writing.

Analyse your days. Create a 24-hour timetable and see where you have the odd half hour spare. Could you spend those few minutes writing? If you take a coffee break or lunchbreak at work, why not find a quiet place to sit and write?

We all enjoy chilling in front of the TV, but wouldn't you be better off filling that time writing your own stories? Of course, it's nice to relax with the family but would they really mind if you had a laptop or notebook on your lap and a pen in your hand?

Discover your favourite 'thinking place'. Possibly, that might be when you're driving or out walking. When I first started writing I seemed to have my best ideas when doing the ironing. So, a notepad on the ironing board was a necessity. And there was always lots of ironing to do. But I would get so wrapped up in my thoughts as I ironed away, I would iron absolutely everything – even socks and pants. But don't panic, you don't *have* to like ironing to be a writer.

Walking however, or some sort of physical repetitive movement aids the creative process. Possibly, exercising the muscles pumps more blood to the brain. Whatever the reason, many writers, including myself, say that walking can help clarify plots, inspire new ideas and really get the creative juices flowing.

If you analyse your day, you will, I'm sure, find a little pocket of free time to call your very own 'writing time'. Once you have set aside a specific time for writing, make that a priority. When you sit down to write – write. (Nappies and squabbles permitting!)

Find time to read

If you can find time to read your favourite magazines, newspapers and novels, why not add 'how-to' books and writing magazines to your home library? Invest in a good supply of 'how to write' books which you can dip in and out of regularly. Whether it's how to write magazine articles, how to write romantic fiction, how to write short stories, how to write for children. Download magazine contributor's guidelines – anything in fact that increases your knowledge about the world of writing. Libraries usually have a good stock of books on writing. If you've a birthday coming up or at Christmas when you're asked what you'd like, why not an annual subscription to your favourite writing magazine?

Get a copy of *The Writers' & Artists' Yearbook* and read the articles as well as browsing the listings. Such books are so informative and inspirational. It will be time and money well spent. The more knowledge you can absorb, the better your writing will become. Enter writing competitions. You have nothing to lose and so much to gain.

When reading fictional novels, as well as enjoying them, also read with the aim of learning from them. Look at the vocabulary; the sentence structure; the dialogue, the description. If a particular scene moved you to laughter or tears or made the hairs on the back of your neck prickle, read it over again and see if you can analyse how the author created this effect.

Inspiration and ideas

Where would we be without inspiration? There would be no novels, no stories, no poetry, no films, no TV drama, no theatre – nothing. The world needs inspiration, and as writers it's up to us to be on the lookout for that illusive flash of inspiration and hold onto it.

Usually, inspiration comes knocking when you least expect it. For example, when you're driving, in the shower, at work, drifting off to sleep etc. So, be prepared with notebook and pens handy; or the ability to record your thoughts onto your phone. You'll have your own methods, but it's never a good idea to rely solely on memory.

If you're struggling to write a single word, write some throwaway sentences. For example, write about the meal you've just had; write about not being able to write; choose an object in your room and write about that; select a word randomly from a book and write what you know about it; look out of your window and write what you can see and hear. This free writing will get your brain ticking and your fingers tapping.

Whatever I write, my first sentences nearly always get deleted. But if I didn't write them, nothing would follow. So, make time to write. Prioritise that time and stick to it.

Important! Don't wait for inspiration or you'll wait forever! Just write something, anything. Free-write,

see where your ramblings take you. There's an old saying – you can't edit a blank page.

Step 2: Tools of the trade

Whenever you get a good idea make a note of it. Ideas tend to vanish as quickly as they come. So, notepads, pens and pencils are your basics to begin with. Even if you plan on writing straight to your PC or laptop, stock up on these essentials. Having your tools on hand all adds to your belief in yourself as a writer. And who doesn't love shopping for stationery and notebooks?

Invest in a good dictionary. While your computer will pick up on spelling mistakes, it may not alert you to the fact that you've used the wrong word. Try not to let mistakes slip through.

A thesaurus is handy but don't be a slave to it. Usually, the first word that comes to mind is the natural one for your own individual style. If you are constantly searching for unusual alternatives, your writing could look forced and stilted.

If you plan on getting published, you need to become computer savvy. You may prefer to write long-hand into a notebook, but at some point, your stories and articles will need to be typed up and saved as a Word document or similar. Publishers and editors tend not to accept hand-written work no matter how neat and tidy it is. Also, while some publications accept submissions on paper through the post, the majority prefer emailed submissions. Check the submission guidelines to see what's required before you send anything off.

An ideas notebook is a good idea. This is the place to store your random thoughts, your flashes of brilliance, all those great ideas. And when you have a brilliant idea, give it a page or a double page all to itself. This allows you the space to jot down additional thoughts as to how you can develop the idea. Ask yourself whether it could be a poem or maybe a short story or flash fiction? Perhaps it would make an interesting article. Could it even be developed into a novel? Jot down all the possibilities for this idea; keep adding your thoughts to this page, and gradually it will become clear what the best way(s) of dealing with it would be.

Handy tools: Have an ideas box or folder in which to keep cuttings, photographs and objects that have caught your eye which might inspire a piece of writing.

Nice tools: A scrapbook or ring binder to paste all your published cuttings in. Picture frames for your published articles or stories – maybe even for your book covers in time.

Useful tools: Small recording device, such as your mobile phone, to record spur of the moment thoughts and interviews. Stock up on stationery, especially sticky notes which are also useful.

You also need a logbook or a spreadsheet to keep track of the written work that you send out. Don't reply on memory.

On your logbook, make columns showing:

- Date sent.

- Title of work.

- Publisher/magazine/competition you sent it to.

- Accepted or rejected, plus date.

- Publication date.

- Amount earned.

- Number of photographs if illustrated.

It's important to keep a record of where you submit each piece of writing for a number of reasons:

- To chase up if you don't hear anything.

- To avoid duplicating submissions.

- So that you know whether to send work to them again.

- To understand their timeframe with submissions.

- For the tax man. If you start earning it must be declared.

- To claim ALCS and PLR payments. (More on these later)

In a nutshell

- Keep an ideas notepad, or a file on your PC or phone.

- You might have notepads and scraps of paper with ideas jotted down, but also have a central file or book where they are logged down. You lose scraps of paper.

- Never rely on memory for flashes of inspiration and ideas. Your brain provides them and then moves on to other important things. So, grab these flashes of brilliance before they fade.

- If you've space for a noticeboard, make it a place to pin photos and cuttings etc. If you do Social Media such as Pinterest or Instagram, you could store inspirational pictures – and draw prospective readers to you and your work. Publishers too maybe? You never know!

- Allow yourself time to be creative. Take a break from your writing to relax and do mundane things. Your creative side will become starved of seeking out ideas and characters and plots and come knocking.

- Absorb yourself in other creative activities and see whether links are formed.

- Take yourself off to somewhere new that might inspire ideas.

- Listen to what other people are doing.

- New places can inspire new ideas.

- Subscribe to online writing sites who send regular links to informative articles and inspirational ideas.

Exercise 1

Free write – for your eyes only, where you see yourself a few years' time, having accomplished some of your writing hopes and dreams.

Exercise 2

Browse the magazines on the newsagents' shelves and online and discover the many different genres and possibilities open to writers. Browse libraries and book shops, look at who publishes what. See what really appeals to you.

Exercise 3

Learn from the experts. Select a page from a professionally published book and literally copy it, word for word, comma for comma. This will give you the feel for sentence structure and punctuation, especially around dialogue. Do the same with a column from a newspaper or magazine. Take note of how every word has earned its place there. Remember to delete your copied work, you don't want to come across it later and think it was yours.

Exercise 4

Set a timer for 5 minutes. Randomly pick a word from a book and write for 5 minutes. Do the same for a second and third word. Finish with one piece of writing incorporating these 3 randomly chosen words. I think you will surprise yourself. Put it aside and polish it later.

Chapter Two:
Solid Foundations

Step 1: Your hopes and dreams

Usually when you think of being an author, you think of writing books. But to embark on writing a book is a major undertaking, especially if you're new to writing. It's a bit like running before you can walk. So why not start by writing something shorter such as a product review, a short story, or a letter to a magazine's letter pages?

When you start writing, just write freely, don't worry too much about perfecting every sentence at this stage. The important thing is to get into the habit of writing regularly. You can perfect things as you learn more about the craft of writing.

Everyone has their own style and method of writing. There are no right or wrong ways regarding how you write. Some people like to write the whole thing before improving, others like to polish and improve as they go along. The main thing is to get something written. Don't become so self-critical that you can't move forward. Remember you aren't writing in stone, so simply get on with your writing, enjoy what you're doing and see how you progress.

So, what are your writing dreams and ambitions? You

may hope one day to write blockbusting sagas, or be a crime writer, or a writer of fantasy novels. You may want to write columns for the women's pages of magazines, or write short stories. Your dream may be to write technical articles for trade magazines. Perhaps you want to write for TV, radio, stage or screen. Possibly, you want to write your autobiography or family history. The world is your oyster, but as mentioned above, my advice is to start small and work upwards, learning as you go. It's an old cliché but a valid one – don't run before you can walk.

If you start off writing something major without first mastering the basics, you are letting yourself in for a lot of rejections and unnecessary re-writing, and success will be a long time coming. You will soon learn that good writing is all about re-writing. You need to edit and polish your work to make it shine. So, avoid giving yourself unnecessary work by making mistakes with the elementary principles to begin with. You need sound, solid foundations on which to build.

Know what you are writing

It helps to know what it is you are writing. Is it a short story, flash fiction, a poem an article, a filler, the beginning of a novel, a radio story, a children's story – and if so, what age range/ability?

If it's an article, what's your purpose in writing it? Is it to entertain, enlighten, educate, amuse, shock, inform? It's useful to know which magazine you are writing it for. If it's a specialist magazine, are you 'qualified' to tell its readers something they didn't know? If it's a general interest piece, have you written it in a lively and entertaining way? If it's a short story, is it for radio or a magazine? Have you checked out what various magazines have space for? Similarly, for radio. What time slots are available?

That all seems like a bombardment of questions, but it really is important to spend some time thinking about what you are actually trying to write.

If it's a novel, have you enough drama to keep readers absorbed for a couple of hundred pages or more? And then what type of novel? Is it a saga, an historical novel, a romance, a crime story, a thriller or maybe a supernatural story? Ask yourself which area of a library or bookshop would this novel sit? That's what publishers will be asking themselves – and possibly you.

If you have a clear idea of what you are writing, and who your intended readership might be, it will help you to focus on producing a good piece of writing.

Step 2: Basic rules of writing

The more you write, the better your writing becomes. Your writing style and techniques will grow stronger as you progress. We are all individuals with our own unique way of writing; no two people will write something in the same way. However, there are some aspects of writing which are universal and need to become second nature to you.

Don't worry, these rules certainly won't restrict your creativity. Basically, they are pretty much common sense and apply to whatever genre of writing you are involved in. But sticking to them as you write will show your skill as a writer and prove that you know your craft.

- Don't waste words: don't waffle or pad out unnecessarily.

- Ensure your spelling, grammar and punctuation are correct; punctuation around dialogue particularly.

- When writing fiction, be aware that too many adverbs can make your work look amateurish.

- Avoid old clichés.

- Use exclamation marks sparingly.

- Never write in stone. Be aware that your first draft is just that, a first draft. Your work will improve with editing and polishing.

- Be correct with your facts: research from reliable sources and double check your facts. If you submit work to an editor containing incorrect information, that editor won't look too favourably on future submissions from you.

- Read your work aloud and listen to the euphony or flow of your words.

- Present your work as neatly as possible and in an acceptable format. Writing for publication is a professional business, so be professional with your approach and your presentation.

Allow these basic rules to become second nature and you'll have plenty of breathing space to be creative.

Step 3: Making a start

My advice to anyone just starting out on the road to becoming a writer is to take it a step at a time. A good starting point is writing a *Letter to the Editor* on a magazine or newspaper's Letters Page.

You might not consider writing a Letter to the Editor as actual creative writing, but this really is an ideal starting point. It's where I started and no doubt it's where many other writers began their writing career. Letters to an editor may be short and to the point but they still require you, the author, to come up with an interesting topic, to craft the sentences skilfully, to write to the style of the publication and present it neatly and legibly. Look on readers' letters as mini short stories or mini articles.

On the positive side, getting a letter published will see your name in print, your thoughts, opinion and cleverly crafted words published, you will possibly be paid for your efforts, and it won't have taken up very much of your time. And believe me, you will be extremely pleased with yourself.

You only have to browse through the numerous magazines and newspapers on the newsagents' shelves to see the wide range of publications that have a readers' letters page. Some pay exceptionally well others just pay for the 'star' letter. Some pay in gifts. Some pay extra for photographs. Others don't pay at all.

Letters to magazines vary in length, style and content, so it is necessary to analyse the sort of letter each individual magazine publishes. Don't assume they are all the same. Some magazines publish handy tips. For example, a gardening magazine might be interested to publish your tip on keeping snails away from lettuces. A lifestyle magazine might like to know how to tell if an egg is still fresh. A motoring magazine might like to know your tips on getting more mileage out of a litre of fuel.

The very first thing I ever had published was a letter to the editor at *Weekend Magazine* many moons ago. It earned me the fantastic sum of £1.50. I cut the letter out and pasted it in my scrapbook. It looked quite lost and lonely to begin with, but not for long.

This is the letter that launched my writing career… *My washing machine had broken, the kitchen floor was flooded. My husband came to the rescue – he bought me a mop!*

Oddly enough my husband was the subject of my next letter too… *I feared romance had died when my husband replaced a photo of me on his dressing table with one of a motorbike!*
It's surprising how you can turn ordinary little incidents

into readers' letters. I once had a vase in the shape of a pair of hands, my letter to the editor was along the lines of my little daughter bringing the vase into the kitchen because I was always saying: "I need an extra pair of hands in the kitchen."

Allow yourself some poetic licence and turn a mundane incident into something entertaining – and get it published.

Before writing your 'Letter to the Editor':

- Study the magazine to discover its readership and their interests.

- Come up with an interesting topic that readers will like.

- Study the published letters and keep within the framework of what is already published.

- Craft every sentence with the greatest care. Make every word count.

- Keep within the word length of previously published letters.

- Write in the style of the publication.

- Present it neatly and legibly.

How to write a 'Letter to the Editor'

Select the journal you want to try for. Read it thoroughly, including looking at the advertisements and photographs. Read the articles and stories and work out what sort of person would buy this magazine. Make sure your writing will appeal to that readership.

Analyse the letters:

- Check the minimum and maximum word lengths.

- Do any refer to something in a previous issue?

- Are any of the letters, handy tips?

- Are any of the letters amusing family/toddler incidents?

- Are the letters controversial or opinion pieces?

- Do letters comment on topical issues?

- Do the letters have accompanying photographs?

- Do the letters have titles?

- Understand why the editor selected these letters.

Once you get a *feel* for the letters published in a particular journal then try your hand at writing something that you believe would slide in very nicely and not look out of place on that page. So:

- Choose your topic and write it as best as you can.

- Now re-read it. Does it have a snappy opening sentence, or a long, unnecessary preamble? Have you made your point or is it jumbled? Is it lively to read or dull? Is it within the word limit?

- Re-write with a more critical eye. Make the opening sentence catchy. Work on the main story so that it is clear. Remove or change dull phrases; make it sharp, lively and easy to read. Ensure it is within the word count.

- Re-write it again making it word perfect. Read aloud or get someone to read it to you and listen. If anything, however slight, jars or sounds awkward, then re-work until you are completely happy.

- Include a relevant photograph.

- Tips for taking photographs for magazines: Make the subject fill the frame so there is no unnecessary background. If you are sending it digitally, send it as a jpg at 300dpi. In your letter, write a brief caption for the photograph.

- When sending your letter include your contact details.

- Jot this submission in your logbook.

How to write a reader's 'Handy Tip'

As with letters, analyse the tips that have already been published, note the word length. Look to see if 'tips' are illustrated with a photograph.

- Choose your topic. You might have your own handy tip, something you've been doing all your life; or you might want to research the subject and come up with something brand new. Maybe you can think of some old wives' tales – the good old-fashioned ways of doing things.

- Look at the readership of the magazine and ensure your tip is appropriate to them.

- Write this up as best you can.

- Now re-read it bearing in mind all the points mentioned. Is it snappy, clear and interesting? Can you include a photograph?

- Re-write and re-write until you are totally happy with it.

How to write a review

Newspapers and magazines publish reviews on all kinds of things: books, plays at your local theatre, restaurant reviews, film and game reviews as well as product reviews. Obviously to write a review, you need to have sampled the product or read the book or seen the show – which is a bonus in itself.

However, before you can put yourself forward to a newspaper, magazine or website to do reviews, you need to be adept in writing them. So, practice. The next time you go to the theatre or restaurant, use a product, play a video game, or read a book, write about it. Trip Adviser is a good platform to write about the places you visit. Amazon is another outlet for product and book reviews. Often, after purchasing something, you'll be asked for your opinion on it. Use this as writing practice.

Be sure to include the facts. If it's a theatre play make sure you cover the name of the theatre, the dates the play runs, running time, who it was written and directed by, who the main actors are, or the ones who really shone. Write your review honestly – but never brutally. The pen is a powerful tool and it's not nice to smash a budding actor's dreams by scathing words. Similarly, for a book review, be honest but never unkind. Remember there is a writer behind that title, and one day that writer could be you.

Once you are confident that you can write a review, do your market research. Study your local newspaper and any local free newspapers, you might find a regular column that publishes reviews. Offer your services (with an example of your style). You may not get paid for your review, but you could get your words published. You may get a regular slot and could even be rewarded with other products and places to review. And when you have a regular outlet for your reviews, there's nothing stopping you from requesting complimentary products from their source to review, which you generally get to keep.

Some journals let you know if they plan on using your letter or review, some don't. Often, it's a case of keeping your eyes peeled for it. An internet search may turn up your published online work. If you've heard and seen nothing after about three months, it's probably safe to assume it hasn't been published, so send elsewhere if relevant and update your logbook. Be aware that if sending a reader's letter to a particular magazine they won't appreciate you sending it to other magazines at the same time.

It is important to keep on writing your letters and reviews. The more you send out, the more chance you have of being published. Once it's sent, get on with the next. Writers keep writing.

In a nutshell

- Have a clear idea in your head what you are writing.

- Understand the basic rules of writing regarding spelling, grammar, punctuation.

- Study what is already getting published in the field that you're trying for.

- Make your writing easy to read and understand.

- Cut out superfluous words and phrases.

- Read your work out loud, develop a critical ear for the flow of your sentences.

- Engage the reader from the start.

- Never be satisfied with your first draft. Polish until it shines.

Exercise 1

Choose a newspaper/magazine that publishes Readers' Letters, Tips or Reviews. Read the magazine from cover to cover, looking at the photographs and advertisements to define who its main readership is. Then, just for practice, write a review about the actual magazine. See if you can post your review on their website.

Exercise 2

Write a reader's letter or a reader's tip to the relevant letters page of that magazine following all the advice given above. Put it aside for a few days. Write up another letter or tip in the meantime. Finally, read your work, edit as necessary and send off. Remember to record in in your logbook. Good luck!

Chapter Three:
Being professional

Step 1: One step at a time

As previously mentioned, you need to know what it is you're writing. What is also important to be aware of, is that when you're writing for publication, there's a lot of competition from professional and experienced writers. Your work needs to be presented in an equally professional manner. The exception to this rule is Reader's Letters. It's okay for them to look 'amateurish'. Nevertheless, they should be legible, concise and have something to say which is relevant to that journal. All other work should be typed and double spaced unless told otherwise. Pages should be numbered, with the title and your name – or an abbreviation of these in the header or footer. For example: W*riter/Evans/30*

When sending work off to an editor or publisher, include a brief covering letter or email. The first page of your manuscript should be a title page. This gives the title of the piece, number of words, your name and contact details. If you're including photographs, here's where you credit the photographer. If sending your work by post rather than email and would like it back, include return postage.

A short item such as a letter or filler, will take a fraction of the time it would take to write a novel, short story or article. But to see your written work and your name in a publication is a huge thrill – and a reason to be proud of yourself. You will be a published writer and there will be no stopping you.

We will be looking at writing short stories and articles later in this book, but to reiterate, I really recommend writing short pieces of work before diving into writing something major. If you concentrate on writing shorter pieces to begin with, you will really get into the swing of writing well and being focused, which is all good practice for your future writing career.

Also, writing shorter pieces to begin with will highlight any areas of grammar, punctuation, spelling and presentation that need to be perfected before you embark on something more time consuming such as a story or novel. The last thing you want is to be making the same basic mistakes over and over again without realising.

In fact, when you get something published, bring up the same piece on your computer and compare the two. While you may read the published piece and be pleased with how great it reads, look to see if the editor has altered anything at all – punctuation maybe, or phrasing. Most likely they will have. Take this onboard and learn from it.

Even if you are only writing for yourself or drafting out an idea, try and think professionally from the start. Never let spelling and punctuation mistakes pass you by. Make it second nature to rectify errors as you see them. If you prefer writing your early drafts onto notepaper rather than a computer, it's a good idea to write on every other line, or every third line. That way you can make changes without your work becoming too illegible.

Step 2: Opportunities

There are lots of opportunities to write short pieces or fillers for magazines. Browse newsagents to see the variety of magazines on offer. This is just the tip of the iceberg. *The Writers' & Artists' Yearbook* lists hundreds of publications. Browse the internet for online magazines, plus trade and specialist magazines.

All of these magazines need their pages filled with articles, stories, letters, tips and fillers. Many magazines offer contributor's guidelines. If they don't, then write and ask what their guidelines are and whether they consider freelance submissions. There are lots of online resources offering lists of paying markets for writers. Do some research and subscribe to the ones you find most useful.

Market research

Make sure you do your market research. Know what magazines want and don't risk your work being rejected because you've sent it to an unsuitable or inappropriate publication. Send your work in good time if it's topical or time sensitive. Monthly magazines usually work at least three months ahead. Weekly and daily papers also work well in advance for features and articles.

People read magazines for a variety of reasons. It might

be for entertainment and relaxation; or to keep abreast of what is going on in their spheres of interest; or to be enlightened and educated in the subject. In fact, people read for any number of reasons. But in a nutshell, people buy a specific magazine because they are interested in its content. So, it is up to you to provide that magazine with something that will interest its readers.

You can work out the type of readership by looking at the content, its style, the adverts and illustrations. Target your work accordingly. If you already read certain magazines regularly you're one step ahead. Consider writing for your favourite magazine.

You can't possibly look at all the magazines out there. So, investing in a copy of *The Writers' & Artists' Yearbook* will be worth its weight in gold. Browse the newsagents' shelves to find magazines that appeal to you. If you are sitting in the dentist's or doctor's waiting room, then spend your time usefully by examining the magazines with a view to writing for them.

Wherever possible, if you want to write for any particular magazine read as many issues as you can. Look at their websites for more information. As mentioned earlier, see if they have contributor's guidelines. Alternatively, analyse the stories, articles and fillers. Look at word length and style. Look to see what sort of titles they use.

Read the small print on the magazine's contents page. This may tell you whether or not they accept freelance submissions. A look at the bylines that is, who the piece was written by, will indicate whether staff writers are providing the content or a mix of freelance writers too.

Step 3: Writing competitions

Keep your eyes peeled for writing competitions. There are so many, from major international competitions, right down to small local ones. Do an internet search for writing competitions and see how many you can find: libraries, festivals, magazines, organisations, writing groups – there are always writing competitions to try for. Plan ahead, and should you find annual competitions which have already closed, note them in your diary in time for next year.

Winning or being placed in a writing competition is a huge boost to any writer's morale. But don't be downhearted if you don't win. It doesn't mean that your story wasn't good or well written. It just may not have been to that particular judge's taste. However, if you have your basics in order, i.e. spelling, grammar, punctuation, presentation, no superfluous words etc., at least you won't be marked down for those reasons.

I've judged many writing competitions, and when there are only a limited number of places to be awarded, it's so hard to have to reject stories which are excellent – but others just have the edge in some way. So, give yourself the best chance by double checking the rules, keep within the word limit, keep on topic and get your entry submitted in good time before the closing date.

If you write to your best ability and you are pleased with the finished result yourself, chances are that someone else will like your work too. Hopefully it will be the judge.

Step 4: Expand your areas of expertise

Writers will often hear the advice 'write about what you know'. But if you are restricted to writing about only what you know, most people's output would be fairly limited. My advice is to write about what interests you. If you aren't an expert in the subject, find someone who is, and talk to them. Read and research the subject until you understand it well enough to write about it. Then off you go! You will be writing about what you know – even if it is only temporary.

Afterwards, there is nothing wrong with asking the 'expert' who you interviewed, if they would read through your article to make sure there are no glaring errors. In fact, if they are being quoted, they will probably be delighted to have the opportunity to read the piece. However, never be persuaded to change your *style* to suit them. You are only asking them to check for incorrect or incomplete facts. Not to write it for you.

I remember interviewing a businessman about his porcelain figurines. He asked to see the finished article. I obliged. However, although there were no errors or anything incorrect with my article, he changed my phrasing so much that it became an advertisement for his company rather than an article.

I knew my editor would not accept it the way he wanted it and I told him so. However, he insisted on having it his way leaving me with no choice but to refuse to put my name to it. The article never got submitted and the businessman missed out on getting his product and his company featured in the magazine.

So, hold onto your standards and be true to yourself. Should you find yourself in a similar situation, discuss it with your editor.

Step 5: Be professional

Writing for publication is a professional business. Your work has to stand up against submitted manuscripts from other professional writers. Give yourself the best possible chance by ensuring your presentation is as professional-looking as anything else the editor may have looked at that day. If you want editors to take you seriously, then your work, your presentation and your approach must be at a professional level.

Study the magazine you plan on submitting to. Find out the editor's name. Address your covering letter or email to them personally, rather than a Dear Sir or Madam start.

While a lot of our communication these days is through email, try to avoid the casual 'Hi' as a greeting – at least until you know the editor. It's perfectly fine to address the editor as Dear Angela, or Dear Mr Jones. Or if you feel that's too formal, then a 'Hello Angela' has a nice touch of respect surrounding it.

Polish your work:

- Do not be satisfied with your first, second or third draft.

- Do not pad with unnecessary words or try to be clever by using obtuse words.

- Ensure there are no punctuation, spelling or grammatical errors.

- If it is fiction, is the punctuation around the dialogue correct and consistent?

- Does your work make sense? Have you tied up any loose threads?

- Be accurate. Are all your facts correct? Is your work trustworthy and reliable?

- Is it neatly typed? Are your pages numbered? Is it double spaced? Is it set out neatly on a A4 Word document with good margins? If printed, is it on one side only of A4 paper?

- Have you included a title page giving the title, your name, contact details and number of words?

- Have you included a brief covering letter?
- Have you read it aloud – covering letter too?

- Are you submitting it to the correct place and person?

In a nutshell

- Present your work as neatly as possible. Writing for publication is a professional business. Give yourself the best possible chance by making your work look professional.

- Make sure you are fully competent in writing shorter pieces before embarking on something more time consuming. You don't want to be making the same basic mistakes over and over again without realising.

- Explore the writing marketplace. See what's out there that you could contribute to.

Exercise 1

Make a list of all the topics you know *something* about. Aim to reach around 30. Then make a short-list of topics you are something of an expert on. Store this list for future reference.

Exercise 2

Write up to 500 words on *one* of the topics from your list. Write it in whatever form you wish, e.g. an article, the beginnings of a short story, flash fiction, a poem – the choice is yours. Put this exercise aside for a day or two then read it aloud. Be sure you read exactly what you have written – not what you *think* you have written. See if you can improve upon it.

Chapter Four:
Aiming for Publication

Step 1: Approaching an editor

Editors are (usually) quite human. They are not demonic
monsters waiting to tear your manuscript – and you, into
shreds. Even so, it can be quite daunting when it comes
to contacting an editor or publisher. The joy of email
takes a lot of the fear away and is probably the best way
of making contact when you have an idea to suggest or a
finished manuscript to send.

Always try and send your enquiry letters or emails to a
specific person. You can usually find names via the
actual magazine or on the publisher's website. When
making contact, be succinct in your covering email or
letter. If it's a short story that you are sending to a
magazine, unless specified, you do not usually have to
send an enquiry letter first. If you have an article or filler
– or you want to pitch an idea for an article, then you do
need to contact the editor.

They don't want your life story – but might want to hear
relevant information about you in connection with this
piece of work, especially non-fiction. And if you're
pitching an idea rather than the finished article, they will
want to feel confident after reading your pitch that you
can deliver.

If you are simply sending in a written piece, editors

generally just want your article/story, neatly presented and a polite, short covering letter. Then be brave, let your masterpiece go. When I'm submitting to a magazine that is new to me, I tend to say in the covering letter/email, that 'I hope they like it and can use at their normal rates.'

If it's a magazine that doesn't offer remuneration, this is their opportunity to let you know. And if they like your piece, it's then up to you whether to allow them to publish your work without payment or withdraw it.

Money isn't always the key issue. If you like the journal, and you'd be quite proud to have an article or story published within its pages, then that may be enough for you, particularly if you feel it's good for your CV. If the topic of your written work really suits the magazine and its readership, again that might be beneficial to you. Make sure you'll be getting a byline i.e. your name to the article. You deserve being credited with your work especially if there's no payment. Additionally, if being published in the magazine opens other doors for you, then I'd say that sometimes these benefits outweigh the monetary side of things.

I would stress however, that if you aren't getting paid for your work, make sure you are benefiting in some way. Let it work for you. If you can see no benefits in letting a journal have your work for free, then hang onto it and look for a market that pays its writers.

Step 2: Pitching ideas to editors

In my opinion and experience, when you've got a great idea for a magazine article or maybe a fictional series, then keep it simple when approaching an editor about it. Firstly, make sure you're pitching your idea to a suitable magazine or publisher. Do your market research first, to be confident that your idea would sit nicely into their pages.

Be clear in what you're proposing: word length, content, whether (if non-fiction) photographs would be included; let the editor know that you're familiar with the magazine and why you feel the readers would like this piece. If relevant, you might want to mention any experts you'll be talking to – or maybe you're the expert in this case. Give the timescale as to when this would be ready to submit to them.

Your pitch might be as simple as a single sentence or two. Or, if you're pitching for a fictional serial or a book or series of books, then your pitch will be more detailed. Be succinct in your outline, make it easy to understand. Putting in too many details can result in a complicated outline that is just too confusing. Importantly, don't promise what you can't deliver.

Step 3: Researching a topic

Whether you are writing fiction or non-fiction, there will come a time when you need to research a subject. These days, internet, research could not be simpler. You can get instant answers by going online. However, look carefully at the source of your information. Make sure it's a reputable trustworthy website; make sure the facts are accurate and up to date. Double check *everything* before using this information in your writing.

Research can be fascinating but it can also hinder your progress as a writer. All that information could bamboozle and bog you down. You may end up trying to fit too much information into your story or article. So, be selective.

Don't just add interesting snippets simply because they are interesting. Make sure they are relevant to what you are working on. Re-phrase your findings to blend with your style. If you slot in as verbatim, they will stand out like a sore thumb, not to mention it being unethical. Absorb the information, re-assemble in your brain and re-write what's necessary in your own unique way.

Books and the internet are great for gathering information, but you can't beat talking to someone who really knows their subject. People generally like to chat about what they are interested in whether it is their work or hobby. So, if you need to know something – ask an expert.

Interviewing someone may sound a daunting prospect and I wouldn't suggest starting with a public figure or university lecturer until you are competent and comfortable with the whole interviewing scenario. (More on interviewing next). However, you may need to know what life was like in the days of your parents or

44

grandparents, so interviewing a relative, friend or an elderly person might be on the cards. Or maybe a character in your story is in a profession that you need to know about. Another good reason for 'asking an expert' is that you get direct quotes and genuine phrasing that will really bring your writing to life.

I worked for 13 years at the *Coventry Telegraph* as a Feature Writer and would occasionally go on press trips. On one occasion I was sent to the Champagne region of France to write about champagne – a dirty job, I know, but someone had to do it.

It was an amazing trip where I explored underground candlelit caverns, vineyards and champagne houses. I spoke to vineyard owners and growers and saw how the whole process of champagne is produced. I got some nice articles from this trip but also, a while later, I was able to use the experience to write a Pocket Novel for DC Thomson which was then taken on by Magna Press as a large print book for libraries.

In *Champagne Harvest* by Ann Carroll (I use my maiden name for romance novels) the words my hero uses in relation to producing champagne, were given to me by those experts in France. The setting, the emotion, the conversations were all authentic and so the book was accepted and still earning me money via PLR. (More on Public Lending Right later).

In a nutshell

- Find out the editor's name and address them personally.

- When pitching an article, serial or book to an editor, keep it simple and uncomplicated. You can go into more detail – if you need to, once you've got their interest.

- Don't promise more than you can deliver.

- Enjoy your research but don't let it bog you down.

Exercise 1
Spend time browsing magazines in newsagents, look at the content and what the editors have to say to their readers. Browse bookshops to see what individual publishers are publishing. Make a shortlist of the ones that interest you.

Exercise 2
Working from your shortlist, check these magazines and publishers on the internet. Look for submission guidelines and contributors' guidelines. Familiarise yourself with the possible opportunities awaiting you.

Chapter Five:
The Art of Interviewing

Step 1: How to interview

You might think you'll never need to interview anyone. Your aim might be to write fiction which will all come from your imagination, no need to speak to anyone at all. But as shown in my *Champagne Harvest* example earlier, there may come a time when you need to know about a type of job you know nothing about or life during an era you haven't experience. You might decide to write your family history and need to speak to relatives. Or you might want to write articles, where talking to experts is often necessary.

If you can develop a good interviewing technique, then you will be able to gather all the information you need for your story or article. However, good interviewing skills need working on so that you can set your interviewee at ease – even your great granny and get them talking. Here are some tips on how to go about this.

Step 2: Preparing for your interview

You need to know in advance what information you need. So, some pre-planning is required. You could almost sketch out the outline of the article or story that you're planning, noting down gaps in your knowledge.

This will help you create a list of questions you need answers for. Write this list in a logical sequence with the first one crafted to put the interviewee at their ease. Be prepared however for the interviewee to surprise you with all kinds of information that you never expected. This in turn, often makes for an even better interview.

Although you have worked out your list of questions, don't expect to stick rigidly to the list, and never recite them 'parrot fashion' oblivious to the interviewee's answers. Simply have them in your head to ask when the right moment arises. It's fine to have a back-up list in your notebook, to double check before the interview ends.

If you are listening to what the interviewee is saying, more questions will spring from their replies. So be sure your questions are open-ended. The last thing you want is 'yes' and 'no' answers. Also gauge how much time you will need for your interview, maybe ten minutes, half an hour, longer? Let your interviewee know what they can expect.

Having a good interviewing technique isn't something that comes naturally to the majority of people. Like everything, it needs to be practiced – so get some practice in before tackling it for real.

There will be so much going on in your head when you interview someone. You're concentrating on what they are saying, you're thinking ahead to your next question, you should also be recording the interview which should include taking notes. Plus, you'll be trying to keep the whole thing on track and not lose your train of thought.

Watch the experts. Get into the habit of watching TV reporters interviewing politicians, celebrities and the general public. See what you can learn from them in their personal approach. Look to see what tactics they use to make the person feel comfortable enough to open up to them. Plus, see if you can spot things that put interviewees on their guard and less responsive.

In my opinion however, watching interviews on TV is actually simpler than when you are conducting an interview for your article or story. The TV presenter doesn't have to write everything down or record it. Someone else is doing that. They aren't expected to take their own photographs either, there's a professional cameraman dealing with that side of things.

If you are planning on writing magazine articles (more on this later) brush up on your photography skills or see if you can team up with a photographer, it makes life a lot easier. But it must be someone who is on the same wavelength as you and can act in a similarly professional manner as you.

I've been so fortunate over the last 30 years of working with a good friend and professional photographer, Rob Tysall of Tysall's Photography. We decided from the very start that whatever we earned would be split 50-50 regardless of whether the article turned out to be picture led or word led. Working as a professional duo, can come across as effective. Plus, it's a lot more fun working with a friend.

Step 3: Recording the interview

Decide how you are going to record the interview. Shorthand is a brilliant way of recording interviews so if you did Pitman's shorthand or Teeline shorthand at college or work, then brush up on it. It's never too late to learn either. I taught myself Pitman's Shorthand using two brilliant books: *Pitman's Shorthand Key to New Course*, followed by *The New Phonographic Phrase Book*. Otherwise, invest in a small recording device or use your mobile phone. Practice using it beforehand, also make notes as you go.

If you are using a recording device or you have your own speed writing techniques, practice reading back from your notebook or recorder, it can be trickier than you might think. I've used a Dictaphone twice in my interviewing career – the first time I pressed the 'pause' button while the interviewee and I had a cup of tea. Sadly, I forgot to press 'record' again when the interview got under way. My second disastrous interview took place outdoors on a blustery day and all I got was the sound of the wind gusting over the microphone. So, practice using your recording techniques before tackling your first real interview.

Be sure to have a notebook and pen as a backup. Never be afraid to ask the person you are interviewing to spell any words that you are not familiar with and always check the spelling of names.

Step 4: Setting up the interview

Make the initial contact with the person or organisation either through an email, letter or telephone call. Explain briefly who you are, what you are writing, what you would like to interview them about, how long you envisage it taking, and whether you are hoping to get it published. Note that I say, 'hoping to get it published'. Don't make promises that you may not be able to keep. If they don't want to co-operate, simply respect that, thank them for their time and leave it. Look for someone else.

If they are agreeable, they might want to talk that very moment, so be prepared for this happening. Alternatively, they might suggest a time when they will phone you or you can call them for a telephone interview. In which case stick to the arranged date and time. Or they might ask you to send questions via email. Make sure you phrase your questions to avoid yes and no answers.

They might suggest you meet up. Obviously be sensible about this and if you are meeting for a coffee it is only polite for you to pay for refreshments as they are doing you the favour. Ask them if they object to you using a recorder. Some people don't like the idea of their every word being recorded. So be prepared with notebook and pencils in case they refuse. Even if you are recording the interview, make notes throughout in case your recorder fails – or you still have the 'pause' button pressed down!

Step 5: Conducting the interview

I've conducted interviews in all kinds of weird and wonderful situations. For example, with a farmer in a field full of buffalo; with a dog handler in an army helicopter doing combat flying; on a fast police launch in the deepest, widest, most turbulent section of the Thames Estuary; I've sat chatting to the owner of a huge mastiff type dog, where the dog has been fascinated by the wiggling of my pen on the notepad and swallowed up not just the pen in its massive jaws but my hand too.

There are always distractions when you interview someone. There was one occasion when I was trying to interview the owner of a blind German Shepherd puppy who was at that biting stage. Rob and I came away from that with rips in our clothing and more than one or two little trickles of blood.

People usually are so nice when you're talking to them about their hobby or work. Often you get invited to have a cup of tea, biscuits, a slice of cake – but don't get too tempted. On one particular job, I'd said yes to tea, then yes to biscuits, then given an antique magic lantern to hold – the subject of the article. And then the interviewee chatted on about the lantern with dates and technical jargon that I needed to write down. The trouble was, I didn't have a free hand to write anything.

But, no matter what the distraction, the only way to gather information from someone you are interviewing is to LISTEN. Also remember that an interview is not a normal conversation where both parties contribute equal amounts of conversation. Although you want your interview to come across as a chatty friendly conversation, in fact you will be listening a lot more than you will be talking. Your input will be to keep the conversation flowing by asking questions; and following on from their comments with further questions – questions which you may not have planned but occur to you at that moment.

Top tips on interviewing

- Begin with a question that puts them at their ease rather than something controversial or too personal. You need to earn this person's trust.

- Do not finish sentences for your interviewee.

- Do not be reminded of when something similar happened to you – and your interviewee ends up listening to your story.

- Don't disagree with their views. (Not out loud at any rate.) And don't wander too far off the subject.

- Do try to nod in agreement rather than verbally agreeing (unless it's a telephone interview). If you are using a recording device your continual 'yesses' may obliterate what the person is saying.

- Do listen carefully and manipulate your questions to follow on from what they have said, rather than reeling your questions off parrot fashion.

- Do look interested.

- If the interviewee tells you something 'off the record' that means it is not for publication. Respect this.

- Do recognise when the interview is reaching its conclusion, and do not drag it out unnecessarily.

- Do thank them for their time. And keep the 'door' open, in case you need to go back to them to clarify something.

Step 6: After the interview

Write up your interview in draft form at the earliest possible opportunity. Write up notes, transcribe the recording. Also, write up your observations about the interviewee, the surroundings, even how you felt about talking to this person. You might not use everything, but it will be in your first draft should you need it.

If an opening sentence springs to mind, write that down immediately, as often, once you get the opening line the rest will flow. Also, be aware that sometimes the concluding sentence your interviewee says will be something quite profound. Maybe it's human nature, but we sometimes subconsciously round things up with a concluding remark that says it all. In my experience it is usually just after you've put your pen and notepad back into your bag.

In a nutshell

- Have some method of recording the interview. Practise beforehand – especially practice reading notes back and transcribing from a recording device.

- Be prepared for the interview. Stick to the arrangements.

- Plan your questions beforehand which might include researching the person or the topic, so you aren't going in totally unprepared.

- When asking questions, be guided by what you're being told, so that your questions come out naturally rather than reeling them off parrot fashion.

- Be friendly, polite and interested. Listen!

- Be well practised in your method of recording an interview and retrieving and understanding your notes.

- Get your interview notes written up as soon as possible in draft form.

Exercise 1

Practising on a friend or family member, interview them on a recent achievement or activity. Be sure you go through all the steps above in preparing for and conducting the interview.

Exercise 2

Write your interview up in full. Then as a practice exercise, or for real, write it up as an article or as part of a story.

Chapter Six:
Writing Magazine Articles

Step 1: The joy of writing articles

I am a big fan of writing magazine articles. I must have written and had published around 2,000 articles on every kind of subject imaginable: animals, sport, food, travel, gardening, business, celebrities, collecting, antiques, miniatures, toys, charities, health, fitness, military vehicles. The list goes on. To give an example of two articles from opposite ends of the scale, I wrote about pine marten poo for *Dog's Monthly Magazine*, (the article was on a dog trained to sniff out the illusive pine marten) and brain surgery for the *Coventry Telegraph's Helping Hands* feature. You can't get more varied than that.

But that's the joy of writing articles. As mentioned earlier, you don't need to be an expert on everything you write about - but you do have to be an expert in amassing the necessary information, having an enquiring mind, speaking to the right people, and being able to expertly reproduce that information in a readable feature for a journal to suit their style and readership.

Your area of expertise is not in the actual subject, but as an expert writer. Your skill is in knowing how to soak up everything about that particular topic and then re-assemble it into a good article for others to read, appreciate and enjoy.

Writing articles has taken me to different countries and behind the scenes in all kinds of organisations. I've met some incredible people including real heroes, celebrities, chefs, actors, people from all kinds of professions and all walks of life. I've been involved in a simulated mountain rescue in Switzerland; I've acted as a 'body' for search and rescue dogs in Scotland, Cumbria and Wales; I've had lunch with arch villains, Darth Vader and Leatherface of Texas Chainsaw Massacre fame; I've had Norman Wisdom sing to me and had an exclusive visit to Charlie Chaplin's home on the banks of Lake Geneva, long before it became a tourist attraction.

Those incidents are just the tip of the iceberg, so many adventures – and all because I write articles. When you're a non-fiction writer it can open up all kinds of amazing opportunities. And, if all goes well, you even get paid for your finished piece of writing once the adventure is over. What's not to like?

Step 2: What exactly is an article?

Be aware of what a magazine article or feature is. It is not an essay or an academic thesis; nor is it a technical report or a fictional story. Your magazine article is the telling of something that will interest a great number of people.

Your style of writing, the approach or angle of the article you've chosen, should attract others to read it. Firstly, it needs to catch the editor's eye and interest him so much that he wants to publish it. It should be accurate, entertaining, informative and lively.

Magazine articles run to all lengths, from a couple of hundred words to many thousands. It all depends on the individual publication.

Magazine editors know their audience They know what their readers would and would not be interested in. They also know what they've covered before.

It's important for you to be aware of the audience too, so that you don't write something for them that is too basic, or too technical, or something that's not telling them anything they didn't already know. When someone has paid out good money for a magazine it's because they are interested in the contents. That might be for relaxation and enjoyment, or to keep up with the news or trends, or it's their favourite pastime or hobby, or perhaps they want to learn more about a subject.

Work out what a reader is getting from spending their time and money on that particular magazine and see if you can supply an article they will enjoy.

Magazine editors constantly need articles that are interesting, original and easy to read. However, because something is 'easy to read' it most definitely does not mean it is 'easy to write'. The opposite is true. In the words of 19th century American novelist, Nathaniel Hawthorne, *"Easy reading is damned hard writing."*

Step 3: Getting paid

Payment for articles varies from one magazine to another. Sometimes you get paid by the number of words – but whatever you do, don't try to pad out your article to increase your fee. No editor wants an article packed with superfluous words. Some magazines have a set fee for contributed articles. Some pay separately for the words and the photographs while some combine the two together.

Some magazines and on-line magazines do not pay at all. Nevertheless, as mentioned earlier, it can be worth going for these markets if it assists your writing career. Many published writers have written for free. It is good for your morale simply to get published and good for your CV.

Step 4: Chicken and egg syndrome

Which comes first? Do you select a magazine that you'd like to write for and then look around for a suitable subject? Or do you write an article because it interests you and worry about finding a suitable home for it later?

Similarly, do you write the article and send it off to an editor, or do you contact an editor and pitch your idea before you set about writing it?

Well., the answer is – it all depends. Every piece of writing is different and there's no hard and fast rule to stick to. If you have a magazine in mind, then look at the magazine's guidelines to start with. See if they accept freelance contributions. There might be instructions as to how they like to receive articles, that is, in full, or to be contacted first with an idea. If there aren't any clear rules for a particular magazine, I would suggest you go right ahead and write the article while you're keen. If it interests you, chances are it will interest others too. Don't risk forgetting about it. Get it written and then look for a magazine to place it.

For me the best thing about writing articles is actually getting out there and researching the topic. I enjoy meeting people and spending time in their world, discovering something that is brand new and different for me. When you write articles, you're never bored. You can't help but become more aware of people, places, activities, hobbies, pets, nature, wildlife – there is so much going on all around you. When you see something that catches your eye, consider how you could write about it so others will enjoy hearing or learning about it too.

Step 5: Article topic

The usual advice is to write about what you know but don't let that limit you. I'd say, write about what interests you. If something has caught your attention, chances are it will interest others too. It pays to be open minded and interested in as many things as possible.

Also, keep your eyes and ears alert to what's going on around you. I remember overhearing a conversation between two men in a pub who were talking about a Russian tank that one of them owned and kept in a barn on his land. I couldn't resist being inquisitive. That was the starting point for an article which earned me £250.

The human element is vital to a good article. Most people are interested in people, so an article just filled with dry factual information will simply be dry and factual. Bring it to life by writing about the people connected to your topic. Your interviewing skills will come into play here.

Keep an 'ideas notebook' to jot article ideas down as they occur to you, otherwise they will undoubtedly drift away. Note each idea down on a separate page, and then add additional thoughts as to how you could use the basic idea. Add in possible marketplaces where it might fit. Think of all the different angles associated with this topic. Keep building up your 'ideas notebook' and before long, you will have more ideas than time to write them up.

Step 6: How to write an article

Once you have decided on the article you are planning to write – and possibly picked out a suitable journal or online magazine where you intend trying to place it, spend some time thinking about how you are going to tackle writing it. You will no doubt find your own way of doing this, but if you are stuck, you could go along this route:

If you have thought well enough ahead regarding what you want to say in your article, you may find yourself coming up with a list of questions that you need answers to. This can help you hone your research down to what is really necessary.

Begin by jotting down the information you already have in no special order. Then do additional research via books, internet, talking to people involved or experts. Get the answers to your questions.

Add your own thoughts to your notes. Eventually you will end up with a higgledy-piggledy mass of information. Then it's time to get it sorted into some kind of order. Think of it like a jigsaw. You have all the pieces – all you need to do it place them into the right order to create a clear picture.

The title:

Although I've started with this, you may not come up with a title until you've written the whole thing. Even then an editor might change it. But basically, the title is the first thing the editor will read. Create a title that catches the eye. Imagine how it will look listed in the contents section or boosted on the front cover of the magazine.

Just recently one of my writing students had another of her articles accepted. The editor got back to her saying: "You had me with the title!" So, don't underestimate the importance of a catchy title.

If you're aiming at a particular magazine be guided by the sort of titles they use. If you are struggling to come up with a title, you could go for a question, a statement, a quotation or a play on words. Here are a few title *types* that I've used in the past:

- A statement: *Turn your junk into jewellery.* (An article on recycling)
- A question: *Who's sleeping with you tonight?* (An article on bed bugs)
- A quotation: *A bird in the hand.* (An article on an animal sanctuary)
- A pun or play on words: *Swims and Needles.* (An article on hydrotherapy and acupuncture)

Standfirst:

This is an opening paragraph that introduces what's coming, often printed in a different font, and often including your name. For example:

Ann Evans goes to meet one man and his amazing tinplate toy collection. (Collector's Gazette)

Usually the editor will write the standfirst, but if they do ask you to supply a standfirst, you'll know what they are talking about. It's usually between 15 and 20 words in length, and basically says in a nutshell what the article is about.

Hook your reader:

You need to grab your reader right from the start, so look for an opening sentence that will really catch their attention. A question maybe, or a bold statement. Once hooked don't let go. Bear in mind the magazine you are writing for and look at their style as guidance. One little ploy is to write in the Second Person using the word 'you' or 'your' in the opening paragraph. Readers tend to become curious if it's going to affect them personally. Try and draw them in at the very start by making the article personal to them.

The body of your article

Now write the story selectively using the information you've gathered to paint a picture of what you want to say. The body of your article or feature should be full of interesting facts, information and possibly personal quotes, all written in a light and lively way.

While you're writing in your own unique style, if you're aiming for a specific magazine, be aware of their style too, and look at what they have published before. Your aim is to get accepted and published – not to re-invent the wheel.

If you have interviewed an expert, select the phrases that really have impact but be careful not to use quotations out of context. Be sure to get the punctuation around quotes correct.

If your article is looking at a topic from various points of view, be equal and fair in stating these opinions via people's quotes. As the writer, you ought to be impartial – give the facts and let the reader make up their own mind. Obviously, this doesn't apply if you are deliberately writing an opinion piece.

Don't feel you have to put everything into one big mass of writing. Articles can be broken up with sub-headings, sidebars and fact boxes.

Your article wants to come across as an 'easy to read' piece, even though you have slogged over it for hours or even days and weeks. Make sure it's logical and interesting. Be sure you've included the major aspects of who, what, where, when, why and how (if relevant). Don't leave the reader feeling puzzled or dissatisfied because you've missed out important aspects. Make sure you've got your facts right.

Ending your article

Be sure you haven't left a major, important point to the very end because sometimes editors or sub-editors will cut from the bottom. They may not realise you were saving the best until last. Get those important bits to the top. Then round your article off conclusively. Don't just let it peter out. You could even link it to the opening sentence, coming full circle. Sometimes all it takes is one small sentence at the end – maybe to cause a sense of wonderment in the reader's mind, or a sigh of satisfaction. Avoid abrupt endings that give the impression of being bored with it all. Finish it off nicely.

Sidebars and fact boxes

These are often coloured boxes in magazine articles set apart from the main body of the article. These are so useful in making your article more interesting and attractive to look at. You can use these for all kinds of additional things. For example, if you are writing about something historic, you could create a timeline of important dates. If it's a foodie article, you could have a recipe here. If you're writing a travel piece, you could list some attractions not to be missed.

Use sidebars in getting across extra information without trying to fit it all into the main body of your article and risk cluttering it. In your manuscript, simply put your sidebars or fact boxes at the end of the main piece. You could number and name them. E.g. *Sidebar 1. Places to visit. Sidebar 2. Best restaurants. Sidebar 3. Further Information.*

Step 7: Editing your article

Whatever you are writing never be satisfied with your first draft. Editing and polishing your writing will improve it enormously but you need to develop a critical eye regarding your own work.

- Make every word count. Your work should not be full of waffle and padding.

- Look at sentence length and make sure your sentences are not too rambling. Short and punchy can be effective.

- Watch out for 'purple passage'. These are over-wordy, flowery piece of writing with too many adjectives, adverbs and clichés.

- Check spelling, punctuation and grammar. Most word processing programmes highlight spelling and grammatical errors, so make use of this facility but don't rely on it.

- Look at the euphony of each sentence and paragraph. Read it aloud and listen to the flow and rhythm. Sometimes, tweaking the punctuation will improve it or the adding or removal of a word.

- Be sure any researched information isn't 'lifted' straight from some other source. Your writing needs to be all in your voice and your style.

- Ask yourself if it's believable and interesting. Does it make sense? Have you covered the topic well? Be sure you haven't left the reader confused or dissatisfied by missing out important elements.

- Is it entertaining or interesting? If you spot any dull areas, re-work them.

- Does it have a great start that hooks the reader and a good, satisfactory ending?

Step 8: Illustrating your article

Plan ahead if you are considering writing on a subject that needs photography and work out it it's going to be beyond your capabilities. The last thing you want is to promise an editor a feature, and then let him down on the photography.

Many people, places and organisations have their own professionally taken pictures which you can gain access to by asking permission. Companies, organisations and tourist attractions generally have a Press Office who will be glad to send you jpg images if you contact them explaining your intentions. Some organisations may want to charge you for using their photographs. Only you can decide whether to take this route.

If you are using someone else's photographs, you will probably be asked to credit the photographer or company for the images. This means you add a note to your covering letter/email when submitting the pictures to the editor saying something like: 'Please credit the photographs to John Smith, XYZ Photography'.

Take note that you can't just help yourself to images off the internet. These are someone else's photographs, so the copyright is theirs. It could land you in big trouble if you used images without the permission of the photographer who took them.

They say a picture paints a thousand words and it certainly is a lot easier to sell an article if it has illustrations with it. If taking your own photographs, then set your camera to its highest dpi. Industry standard is 300dpi. Most people would work on automatic but with some photographic education, understanding shade, depth of field and focusing can make your finished article acceptable or even excellent.

Send in a selection of photographs if possible so the editor has a choice. Usually, magazines accept photographs as jpgs. Most magazines accept submissions by email, but if you're planning on sending a number of jpgs, then the recipient might appreciate them being sent by WeTransfer, Dropbox or similar, rather than filling up their email inbox.

What I tend to do if sending an article and images to a magazine new to me, is to make low-resolution copies of my photographs (72 dpi) – I use the free system GIMP to do this. I can then send some small images with my article via email which allows the editor to see what's on offer and make a decision. Once you've got the okay, you can send your high res images via Dropbox, WeTransfer (or similar).

Always caption your photographs, either re-name the photo with your caption or make a list of captions at the end of your article. For example:

DSC 0023: Sculptress Mary Green with her life-sized cardboard model of a unicorn.
DSC 0024: Artist John Brown with his painting of an ostrich.

Sometimes, facts that haven't made it into your article can be incorporated as a picture caption.

The first article I ever had published was in *Nursery World* magazine and called 'Room for One More'. As a young mum at the time, it was about how not to make your older child jealous when a new baby comes along. I didn't know about sending photographs with articles then – no one had told me. So, when I saw they had included a photo of a little boy and baby girl, I realised I could have sent a photo in – lesson learnt.

Step 9: The professional approach

Whether your writing is targeted towards a top glossy magazine or it's an ode to your dog, you need to present it as perfectly as possible. And while your dog will love you whatever you do, magazine editors are not so forgiving. So, if your writing is to stand the best possible chance of being read, accepted and published, then it needs to look professional.

Editors receive many hundreds of manuscripts every week. Undoubtedly, many of them are carelessly presented – much to the frustration and annoyance of the editors who are *actually looking* for well written pieces of work suitable for their publication.

Maybe an editor will be willing to struggle through badly presented work in case there is a hidden gem there, but chances are they might just give it the briefest of glances and reject it purely because they have not the time nor the inclination to re-work the piece even if it is fairly good. After all, if the author couldn't be bothered, why should they?

It's vital to give your work the very best chance by making it stand out from the crowd by its professional presentation. Simply neat, legible and concise – and of course, well written.

Many magazine editors appreciate an enquiry letter for ideas you may have for articles and features. This helps them plan ahead, and of course it is far better for you to know whether an editor is interested before you have gone ahead and written it. But, as mentioned earlier, the *chicken and the egg* syndrome springs to mind. Personally, I've written hundreds of articles because the subject interested me, then gone in search of a suitable magazine.

When contacting an editor with an article proposal, know that your writing skills start here. If you send a dull, boring or poorly thought out enquiry letter, they might assume the article itself will be dull, boring and poorly thought out. It might be pertinent to say why you feel 'qualified' to write this article. For example, perhaps you've studied the subject, or you're involved in some way. Or maybe you plan on talking to an expert.

You could ask whether your suggested length for the article is suitable or ask for their preferred number of words. Be flexible on word count. Never write in stone. Editors like to be able to work comfortably with a writer and one who would not dream of altering one of their precious words is unlikely to get many editorial commissions.

It's fine to ask what the payment is for freelance contributions. Alternatively, as mentioned earlier, offer the article to them 'at their usual rates'. You could offer to send the article on spec, which means you are not asking them to commission you in advance for the article, but you would be happy to write it and send it in the hope they will like it and use it.

Just to reiterate, as with any piece of writing, go over your enquiry letter checking for errors and spelling mistakes and to ensure you have put your suggestion over in a manner good enough to attract an editor.

Presentation

Your work must be neatly typed, double spaced, pages numbered with a word from the title, your name or surname and page number. I tend to do this in the header in a smaller font. E.g. *Become/Evans/72*. Save your work as a Word Document or similar. Include a title page which shows the title, word count, your name, contact details, photography credits. This sits as the first page of your manuscript. Send as an attachment to your email.

If you aren't sending by email, then print on one side of A4 white paper. Check with the editor, or the submission guidelines to see whether they prefer to receive manuscripts by email or print.

Step 10: Let your published articles earn you extra

Once you start having articles published, so long as the magazine you're published in has an ISSN number (International Standard Serial Number) you can log your published work – print or digital, including your published images (providing you own the copyright) with ALCS or DACS who will collect and distribute royalties due to you for the re-use of your work. Visit their websites for more details.

ALCS – Authors' Licensing and Collecting Society.
https://www.alcs.co.uk/

DACS – Design and Artists Copyright Society.
https://www.dacs.org.uk

In a nutshell

- Know that magazine articles come in all shapes and sizes.

- Study magazine's 'Contributor's Guidelines' to know what's required.

- If your article is for a specific magazine, study that magazine.

- Plan your article and give it structure.

- Hook the reader with the first sentence.

- Make use of Sidebars and Fact Boxes.

- Understand how to use photographs to illustrate your article.

- Edit and polish to ensure a professional piece of work.

Exercise 1

Study a few magazine articles and work out the author's

thought processes. Consider how they must have gone about it to achieve the finished product. Ask yourself why the editor accepted that article. Now plan to write a 750-word article on a topic of your choice. Refer back to your original list of things you know about. Target your article towards a suitable magazine that you are familiar with. Do whatever research is necessary.

Exercise 2

Write your article remembering to include (if relevant) quotes, sidebars, fact boxes, further information sources etc. Put the article aside for a day or two then read aloud and polish until it is word perfect. Type it up as professionally as possible, include a title page and a brief covering letter, check and send. Record it in your logbook.

Chapter Seven: Writing Fiction

Step 1: Finding ideas for stories

Before you can embark on a story you need at least the spark of an idea. That spark might come in the shape of a character, some real life happening, a theme, an emotion, an overheard remark, a dream, a nightmare, an object, a photograph – anything in fact. For me, buildings very often spark an idea – derelict buildings in particular seem to fire my imagination. At least two of my 30 plus books were inspired by the crumbling ruins of abandoned, derelict houses.

An old photo at Blackgang Chine on the Isle of Wight of a house on a clifftop shortly before it crumbled into the sea inspired my third children's book, *Disaster Bay.* And a ramshackle old house I used to drive past on trips to Leicester inspired the house where my protagonist in *Kill or Die* gets held hostage.

There's nearly always a spark of truth behind all of my books. Some link with a real event, a place or person that has got me writing. These sparks range from the tiniest of incidents to major events. Here's a few of my inspirational moments:

My brother buying an abandoned canal boat resulted in *Fishing for Clues*. Driving past open-curtained windows at night inspired me to write *Pushing his Luck.* A music concert led to *Stealing the Show*. A man walking down my street inspired a short story called *The Magic of Christmas*. A newspaper headline prompted me to write *The Uninvited* a vampire themed YA book. An ancient church inspired YA thriller, *Celeste*. A crushed coke can inspired my first reluctant reader book, *Nightmare*. A visit to a little Scottish museum inspired my award-winning children's book, *The Beast*. A newspaper delivery boy got me writing *Pointing the Finger*; a friend's childhood memory inspired award-winning reluctant reader book, *A Little Secret* and the list goes on. Anything can spark an idea. The trick is to catch hold of that spark and hold onto it until you can develop it into something more substantial.

Inspiration very often comes when we aren't looking for it. Ideas can flit in and out of our heads at any time of day or night. Make sure you have ideas notebooks dotted around your home to write those ideas down before they are lost to you. Keep a box or folder where you can store cuttings and photographs which might be used in some way in your stories. And of course, have files and folders on your PC where images of people and places can be stored for later use.

Step 2: Developing ideas

It only takes a spark of an idea to inspire you to write. But a spark is not a story, so how do you expand a spark into a fully-fledged story?

We all work in different ways. An idea might develop and germinate in your head over days, weeks, months –

even years. You might find it easier to get notes written down on paper or computer, where you can expand on them and let the imagination take over.

With luck your idea might unfold itself from start to finish with a logical string of events and action that simply needs writing down. On the other hand, it could be a confusing jumble of images and thoughts with no clear path in sight at all.

Perhaps your idea is the ending. You visualize a scene crammed full of action or emotion, but you have no idea of the events or characters that have led up to this point.

So basically, you have a spark of an idea which will not be ignored. From this point you need to expand on your idea. You need to develop a storyline and to do this you need to create characters. It may be that your characters have introduced themselves to you in your head already. Perhaps a character was the initial spark. Either way, spend time thinking about them and getting to know them. (More on characters later.)

Perhaps the setting for your story was your inspiration. If so, learn more about this place, research and explore, gather photographs of it. It's fine to collect images from the internet for your own personal use.

The spark for my 'Beast trilogy' (*The Beast, The Reawakening* and *Rampage*) came when holidaying in Scotland. Sunlight sparkling off the mountain tops kept catching my eye making me think I could see something up there. But when I looked there was nothing. That was my spark of an idea which I began developing. *Maybe there is something up there, watching…*

In my head I came up with lots of 'what ifs'. What if it's a dangerous animal living in the mountains? What if it's growing angrier by the second and decides to stalk some unsuspecting holidaymaker? What if… and so on. Once I had decided there was definitely something up there in the mountains which was decidedly dangerous, the actual revelation of what that creature/character was, came about when I visited a little museum on that same holiday and saw the skull of a particular type of animal. (No spoilers as you might want to read the books yourself.)

Development of the story was then well under way. But, had I not held onto the initial spark of the idea, these books would never have been written.

So, treasure those inspirational sparks and ideas, and store them safely where they won't get lost. Develop them into something special and enjoy the process.

Step 3: Conflict

Your story needs conflict. If you don't have conflict, then you don't have a story. There must be problems for the protagonist to overcome. Even the gentlest of stories needs conflict, including children's stories. Glance at picture books and you'll find the main character is trying to do or achieve something, even if it's just looking for their teddy's lost ear.

Conflict does not mean all guns blazing and people at war with one another. Conflict comes in all different forms. There is inner and outer conflict – or emotional and physical. Inner (emotional) comes from a character's own moral standing, their beliefs, background, upbringing, personality, etc.

Examples of emotional conflict: perhaps it involves your main character doing battle with their conscience over something. Or the conflict may revolve around your character loving someone. It might be that your character is extremely anxious about a forthcoming event. Conflict is a word that encompasses the character's problems, troubles, difficulties, insecurities, worries, and anxieties.

Outer conflict (physical) comes from difficulties arising which are beyond their control, such as other people, the weather, physical obstacles, health issues. Your story *must* have conflict. Your protagonist's difficulties are what keeps the reader reading on.

Basically, give your character a big problem to overcome and don't let them get out of it too easily. By the end of your story your character should have either overcome their problems – or not.

Or maybe they will have got to grips with their problems. But even if they haven't, try and end on a note of hope that at least they have learned something by the experience. Don't leave your reader feeling dissatisfied by the outcome. If your story has a number of sub plots make sure these are all wrapped up. Avoid leaving lose ends.

Two quick tips

If you're stuck for a story idea, try this: Give your character a goal – something they are trying to achieve. It doesn't have to be complicated. Perhaps a new bride wants to cook a meal to impress her in-laws. Next, think of obstacles to spoil her plans. Maybe the cooker breaks down, or she burns everything, or she adds salt instead of sugar to the dessert. You have a story.

Or, give your character a fear – something they really struggle to cope with. Now create a situation where they have no choice but to face that fear. How will they cope? As an example, let's say your protagonist is new to the area but has been invited to a party with her child. They are both delighted – the chance to make new friends. However, she has an irrational fear of clowns – coulrophobia. And wouldn't you know it, a clown has been booked as entertainment for the kids. Does she face her fear or give in to it and pass up the chance to make friends? It really matters to that character – and you have a story.

Simple ideas but make the consequences important to your character. Come up with twists and surprises but these basic scenarios can be used time and again, and the stories made as in depth and complicated as you wish. It's just that little spark you need to get going.

In a nutshell

- Keep ideas notepads and use them. Have an ideas box or folder to store things in which might inspire you. Have an ideas folder on your computer.

- Never rely on memory for flashes of inspiration and ideas. They vanish swifter than they arrive. Grab those flashes of brilliance before they fade.

- If you've space for a noticeboard, make it a place to pin photos and cuttings etc. If you do Pinterest, you could store pictures and sayings on there. It might also draw prospective readers to your page and your work. Publishers too maybe? You never know who is out there watching.

- Allow yourself time to be creative. Take a break from your writing to relax and do mundane things. Your creative side will become starved of seeking out ideas and characters and plots - and come knocking.

- Absorb yourself in other creative activities and see whether links are formed.

- Take yourself off to somewhere new that might inspire ideas. New places – new ideas.

- Listen to what other people are doing.

- Read books and magazines on writing; subscribe to free online writing sites who send regular links to articles and inspirational ideas. At the time of wring here are a few current ones:

writers-online.co.uk., Reedsy.com, script-consultant.co.uk., Authors Publish Magazine. There are many more.

Exercise 1

Choose a place you know well, allocate a season of the year to it. Now place a character into that setting. They are feeling one of these emotions: sorrow, joy, fear or anger. Free write on this scenario, see if you can come up with the reason the character is feeling that way. See the situation through the character's eyes.

Exercise 2

Write for 10 minutes on something that happened to you yesterday. After 10 minutes introduce a fictional element to your story – something that takes the story off into a new direction. See where you can go with this.

Chapter Eight: Developing your writing style

Step 1: Developing your own unique style

If you look at the great writers of the past, names which spring to mind might be William Shakespeare, Charles Dickens, J.R.R.Tolkien, Jane Austen, Mark Twain, George Eliot or any of the other classic writers from long ago. There is no doubt that these writers were great, their work has withstood the test of time. But as they picked up their pens – or quills in some cases, they probably never imagined their stories would still be being read centuries on. I imagine, as they sat down to write they were feeling just as apprehensive and uncertain about getting their thoughts and ideas down on paper, as any novice or experienced writer of today.

Of course, these days, with more opportunity to know what's going on in a writer's head through social media, blogs, articles etc., we learn that even the most famous, experienced writers have their off days and writing hang ups. Nevertheless, writers whose work we know and admire have all persevered and eventually completed their work, surmounted their difficulties and got it published.

Think about your favourite authors. If you analysed why you enjoy their books so much, what would you say?

- They write a cracking good tale.

- The plot is always believable yet full of unexpected twists and turns.

- The characters seem like real people who you become involved with.

- Stories are full of suspense, impossible to put down.

- Their writing is beautiful – simply a joy to read.

- Their descriptions paint vivid scenes in your mind.

- The stories are full of emotion, making you laugh and cry.

- The stories are thought provoking.

Whatever it is about the way an author has captured your interest, it is unlikely that you would say: "I liked this book because it reminded me of a book by so-and-so."

Stories you enjoy have all been written in that author's own style, their own voice. They have written it in the way that was natural to them.

Reading is important to writers. Analysing the way certain authors write their stories can be a useful lesson in creativity, but to try and imitate their style is pointless. However, the public could be waiting for *your* book, written as only *you* can – in your own inimitable style.

So, when considering your style don't fret because you'll never be able to write like Charles Dickens, Agatha Christie, Stephen King, J K Rowling or any other famous name – because no one expects you to, and no one wants you to. Your style will come from you, and only you. It will be *your* unique style.

Publishers say they are looking for originality – therefore *you* have what they need. We are all unique in our own way. There is no one else quite like you. No one thinks or acts or writes like you. So, if you write in your own style, being true to yourself, that originality will shine through.

However, you won't find your own style by thinking about it too much – you find it by writing. The more you write, the more your style will develop. You may not even notice that you have a particular style, but others will. However, your style must constantly be worked at and improved upon by learning the craft, writing and re-writing.

If your style is to simply write the first thing that comes into your head and leave it that way, then it will be your own style, but it probably won't be anything special. Re-writing and editing your work is as important as getting it down in the first place. If you do not work at getting the very best from your writing, then you are not being true to yourself, and success will be a long time coming.

Step 2: Improving your style

To write good fiction, it is essential to understand basic

grammar and punctuation. Reading your work aloud will help you to identify any incorrect grammar so that you can rectify it.

Punctuation

Incorrect punctuation is annoying to readers and editors alike. Although a story should get a thorough line-edit before being published, the writer should ensure their writing is up to an acceptable standard in the first place. Don't take it for granted that someone else will correct your mistakes. Writing is a professional business, so give yourself the very best chance by presenting your work as professionally as possible. And that means getting your punctuation correct.

Also, remember that how you punctuate your writing will either make it flow beautifully or not. It will either become a joy to read or a jerky, uncomfortable experience for the reader. The correct punctuation will also ensure you achieve the desired pace and mood that you want. Incorrect punctuation can also change the meaning. These examples will make you smile:

A woman without her man is nothing.
A woman: without her, man is nothing.

"Let's eat Grandpa!"
"Let's eat, Grandpa!"

Be particularly careful with punctuation around dialogue. Remember ALL punctuation goes inside the speech marks.

"Are you sure about that?" he asked.

"Yes, absolutely!"

"Hey, shouldn't that be a capital *h* on the word *he*? It does follow a question mark."

"Nope! If you're adding a speech tag it's lower case if following any punctuation mark except a full stop. If you end the dialogue with a full stop, you wouldn't add a speech tag. Your next piece of narrative would start a new sentence with a capital letter." With a sigh, she read what she'd written and moved on.

Paragraphs

There are no hard and fast rules as to the length of a paragraph. Basically, just as a sentence centres around one statement, then a paragraph elaborates on that idea. Once that has been dealt with a new paragraph begins. Of course, when writing fiction and you have characters talking to one another, start a new paragraph every time you write a new piece of dialogue from a different character. (More on dialogue later).

Also, vary those paragraphs. If your page is a continuation of short paragraphs, it could become irritating to the reader. Or if it is one big chunk of words without a break, it could become boring and unappealing to the eye.

Be aware that fiction is usually set out differently to non-fiction. Study published fictional stories to see how new paragraphs are usually indented.

Clichés

Be careful that familiar expressions and clichés don't creep into your narrative. Things like: *It was as black as night; it was as old as the hills; she was no spring chicken.* If you find yourself using expressions that you're heard many times before, delete them and come up with a new way of describing something. Your style will not benefit from churning out old clichés. If you want to use similes and metaphors, create your own unique ones.

Adjectives

Be careful with adjectives. Too many, too frequently, can be irritating and seem amateurish – select them with care. Look for ways of narrating your story without littering it with adjectives. The result will be far more alive and colourful than you would ever have imagined.

Adverbs

While you might think adding adverbs to enhance your dialogue will improve your work, the opposite is often the truth. Use adverbs sparingly. It's too easy to add an adverb to a speech tag, thinking you're adding to the effect. But this could be making your work appear amateurish. E.g. *John said happily; Mary answered angrily.* Let the dialogue speak for itself without having to tell the reader how it was said.

Vocabulary

When looking for the correct word to use, choose the most natural sounding word that comes instantly to mind. Avoid searching for pompous or obscure alternatives – they won't impress anyone. But on the other hand, if a long or obscure word is the correct word to use in the circumstances, then use it with confidence.

Step 3: Read your work aloud

Always read your work aloud and listen to the poetry or euphony of each sentence. If your sentences sound awkward or ugly, then re-write them, it might only be a matter of a slight re-arrangement, or the addition or deletion of a word or comma, but it may make all the difference to how your work sounds.

What helps to make your style unique is that we all have different experiences in life and different opinions. As we write, we draw on our experiences, weaving those memories and emotions into the thoughts and actions of our characters – sometimes deliberately, sometimes subconsciously.

Our knowledge of the world and its inhabitants reveals every possible human trait: the anger, jealousy, love, hate, friendships, betrayal and so on. What we haven't experienced personally, we will have seen on TV, read about in newspapers and witnessed through other people's actions. Our take on all these things can be portrayed through the way we write our stories.

So, whatever your style, make sure you produce smoothly written work, which is easy to read, without spelling and grammatical errors. You can have metaphors and similes, if you wish – but as mentioned earlier, make them *your* unique metaphors and similes, not old clichéd ones.

Your style should feel natural to you, rather than trying to emulate your favourite author. Your style shouldn't come across as trying to impress with the vocabulary you use. I'm not saying a thesaurus doesn't come in handy at times, but words searched for from a thesaurus rather than taken from your own stock of words in your head, will probably stick out a mile.

Remember, no one can create that style for you. It's individual – unique to you. And the more you write, the more your style develops.

In a nutshell

- Be yourself when writing, don't try to imitate another writer.

- Understand the basics of good writing, regarding grammar, spelling, punctuation and so on.

- Avoid being a slave to the thesaurus. Have confidence in the words that come instantly to mind.

- Read your work aloud and listen to the euphony of it.

Exercise 1

Free write for the next three minutes, without any pre-thought, on one of these topics: your pet; your job, your hobby; your house or your garden.

Exercise 2

Read what you have just written and save for future reference. Now re-write, looking to re-phrase or bring in more colour, life and emotion. Having made a start, could you write more on the subject? Keep writing and see where it leads you.

Exercise 3

Check your punctuation and see if you have created an easy to read passage. Read it to yourself, pausing *only* where you have put a punctuation mark – not when *you* need to take a breath. Listen to the 'poetry' or euphony of each sentence and adjust so that each sentence flows.

Chapter Nine:
Creating Believable Characters

Step 1: Bring in your characters

Where do all those amazing characters that we've met in stories come from? Do writers use people they know in real life, or simply conjure characters up from thin air? Ask any author how they created their characters and you'll get a multitude of answers. Often, the author can't say exactly where they came from. Some just seem to jump into the author's mind and demand to be written about. Other characters emerge more slowly, as the author begins to write, discovering more about them all the time.

Some appear speaking words, acting out scenes and behaving in a way that the author has no control over. If that happens to you, be grateful and get everything written down as quickly as possible. Maybe you'll find that you create characters by writing a character description about them, covering their appearance, personality, background and so on.

We will automatically draw on our own experiences and people we know or are acquainted with; even strangers and passers-by in the street can often spark an idea for a character.

A word of warning about basing a fictional character too closely on a real person, as this might hold you back when it comes to creating conflict for this character. You might not be able to take things to the extreme if you've got, for example, your grannie or best friend at the back of your mind.

Also, no matter how well you think you know someone, you can't know their every thought, every action, every hope and dream. And you *need* to know all of these things and more if your characters are to appear real. It's a similar situation when writing in the first person, the 'I' character, really does need to be a character in their own right.

Don't be fooled into thinking that writing in the first person is the simplest option because it's *you*. If you're thinking of the character in your story as yourself, you aren't likely to push the boundaries beyond your own experiences, and that might not make for a great story. After all, would you really want to put yourself through danger, disaster and heartache as your protagonist will probably endure? Obviously, draw on your own experiences, beliefs, emotions and so on, but let that character have an independent existence and not be a reflection of you.

Step 2: Get inside your character's head

Stories are all about characters. We create them, give them lives and backgrounds, then place them in situations where they find themselves in some sort of difficulty – emotional, physical or both. The story then is how they react to the problems facing them.

As writers, it's our job to keep the reader engaged as the character works through their problem. Somehow, we must make that character interesting enough for the reader to care what becomes of them. If your character is one-dimensional, wooden, or nothing but a caricature, then the reader probably won't be bothered one way or the other. Or if you as the writer haven't allowed the reader to really get to know the character, that won't hit the mark either.

So firstly, your characters need to be real three-dimensional people who the reader – and you as the writer, really believe in. Secondly, and most importantly, you need to write through your main character's (your protagonist) viewpoint. That is, writing as if you are that person. The world is perceived through *their* eyes and emotions – not yours.

As the writer, think of yourself as a puppeteer. You're sitting back in your chair pulling the strings at arms' length. You create the characters and then set them free in this fictional world which you've also created and see what happens.

As the writer, you remain operating those strings. If you let go, the characters and the story will collapse. It's just that you must stay well out of sight, so you've giving the illusion that the characters are standing up for themselves.

When it comes to the narrative, that is, where you're setting the scene, describe it in a way that's in tune with the atmosphere of the story, and the mood and emotions of the character at that moment.

Step 3: Caring about characters

It's so important that the reader cares about your characters. If they don't, they aren't likely to read on. So, for readers to care, *you* must care about the characters you create. You have to believe in them and be intensely involved with them.

To be honest, this rapport with your characters isn't an immediate thing. Usually this bond develops as you write, as those characters start talking in the dialogue and reacting in the narrative – when they start thinking and acting for themselves. Often, it's only as you get into the story that their true personalities emerge, and sometimes in ways that surprise you. Perhaps you'll discover their changing moods, their fears, their humour – or lack of it, what spurs them on, what they love and what they can't stand. Often you will discover skills that you never knew they had – yet turn out to be important later in the story.

On the other hand, as you get well into the story, you might realise that certain aspects are missing. Then it's a case of going back to the beginning and blending in the important details you need for later. But that's the great thing about writing, you aren't writing in stone. You can go back over those early parts of the story and re-write, once you know your character better.

Step 4: Visualise your characters

Before you can write anything, you need to see your character in your mind's eye, even if it is just a vague image to begin with. Once you start to write about him or her, they will become much clearer to you. Gradually, as you get to know their background, their skills, their personalities, their fears, their dreams and so on, they will start to become real.

As you start to colour in your sketchy outline and fill in the blanks, your character will become a living, breathing person with a mind and opinions of their own and with a background and a life that involves others. It's worthwhile to spend time writing a character sketch for each of your characters. This would be just for your own reference, don't even try to include all these points in your story.

- **Appearance:** Gender, age, height, shape, colouring, hair style, nationality, clothing; mannerisms, gait, habits. The way they speak and move. What's their own opinion on how they look? Do they see themselves as others see them?

- **Normal life:** Where they live; marital status, their work; education; birth date, star sign, intelligence; financial situation; hobbies and interests; family circle; friends; relationships; enemies; skills; fears and phobias; favourite things; likes and dislikes; aim in life.

- **Personality:** Here's a few traits to consider: Shy, outgoing, talkative, quiet, moody, cheerful, optimistic, pessimistic, depressive, revengeful, timid, thoughtful, thoughtless, kind, unkind; forgiving, unforgiving, sense of humour; calm, easily angered. What's their opinion on political issues, religion and topical issues?

- **Background:** Past experiences shape a personality, just as their current situation affects their moods and behaviour. Make sure your characters have solid backgrounds.

As well as knowing your characters, you also need to understand them. It is not enough to have characters simply disliking one another, there has to be a reason behind this. Similarly, don't expect the reader to believe two characters are in love, or falling in love just because you say so. This must come across through their interaction, thoughts, dialogue and emotions.

A fun way of really getting to know your characters, is to make a list of random questions to ask your character. For example, what do they keep hidden in the box at the bottom of their wardrobe? When did they last cry? When did they last laugh? What secret do they hope never comes out? Their answers will surprise you.

Probably only a fraction of your character sketches and traits will come to light in your story, but if you know all this and more, your character will be real to you, true to themselves and believable to the reader.

Step 5: Nobody's perfect

Nobody's perfect – although I'm sure a few people will disagree. But at least when you're writing fiction, you don't want perfect characters. It's often the flaws and the imperfections that make our characters unique and interesting. Also, perfect characters aren't likely to get themselves into situations that are worth reading about. However, you're trying to create characters who the reader will empathise with, and not find annoying or pathetic. It's a fine balance.

There are so many personality flaws that our characters *could* suffer from, so spend time considering the complexities of their personalities. Obviously, there are some that certainly would never fit into your 'hero' category. For example: being cruel to animals, old folk and children; or being a bully. Save those traits for your villains.

By giving your character flaws and weaknesses – and you as the writer *knowing* how these have come about, you will create believable, interesting characters. It's that *knowing* on your part that will make or break the believability

While we need characters to 'stay in character', they can be contradictory in their behaviour if the right circumstances come about. Also, people behave differently depending on who they are with or talking to. So, your protagonist has flaws and weaknesses. If you plan on bringing them to the fore at some major turning point in your story, it might just seem that they are acting out of character, which the reader won't appreciate. The solution would be to hint at such flaws before they appear. Be subtle in your handling of this as you don't want to alienate the reader.

For example, showing your protagonist with a furious temper could turn some readers instantly off. Unless of course you show it when he or she is angry about someone being unjust to someone else.

Jealousy isn't an attractive trait, but your protagonist 'beating themselves up' about feeling ridiculously jealous, as they try not to be, reveals their flaw but could also be endearing to the reader.

Then, there's the baddies and villains of your story, who you want the reader to feel strongly about. Reveal their unpleasant traits in whatever way you find effective. No need to show them in a good light. Just be sure to show them in their true light. Let the reader see how they are behaving and make up their own mind.

When creating a dislikeable character, have them behaving in ways that will get some sort of emotional response from your reader. The last thing you want is the reader shrugging their shoulders having no interest in them at all. Make the reader so irate that they must keep reading in the hope that the 'baddie' gets what's coming to them.

So, have fun with flaws and weaknesses, and make sure your characters are complex and interesting enough to keep the reader right there – reading.

Step 6: Motivation

"What's my motivation, darling?" said the actor to the director. The actor given the part, wants to know the back story; what's been going on; what their character's aims, intentions and ambitions. The reason the actor needs to know is so they can portray that character with real depth and meaning. As writers, we are the directors of our stories. And it's important that we know the motivation behind every single character – whether they have a walk on part, or the starring role.

If you aren't clear on each character's motivation, then your reader won't be either. Without motivation, your characters could be inconsistent in their behaviour and attitude. A clear motivation will make them a stronger, more believable character. They know exactly what they want and are determined to achieve it. When you have two characters strongly motivated, that's when conflict occurs, and your story becomes character led rather than plot led. Give your character a strong, realistic motivation and your reader will understand them, even if they don't empathise with them.

Every character in your story should be feeling motivated in some way. The fact that you have created them and given them a role in your story, means that they have a background, family, friends, dreams. Maybe their motivation is just to get on with their job at this point in your story when they come into contact with your protagonist. Maybe they are reacting to something that's happened in their lives, and it might impact on your character. Only you can decide.

Your characters' motivations will reveal a lot about them such as their moral standards, their beliefs, their values, their strengths and weaknesses, as well as their hopes, dreams and fears. Every single character in your story has a reason for doing what they do. Take time to examine their personalities and circumstances – and get them motivated.

Step 7: Naming your characters

Finding the right name for your characters is important, and you'll know from your own experience that different names conjure up different images. If you're one of those writers who can't continue until they have the right name for their characters, could I suggest you try and put this aside; give them a temporary name rather than let it stop you from progressing.

Remember that names can be lengthened or shortened, which is worth thinking about, as this can show the mood of other characters or reflect the atmosphere of the scene by the way one character addresses another.

Although the popularity of names can indicate the timeline, the era, social class and a lot more, names do come around in circles, but beware of modern names. Be sure the name would have been around when your character was born. The internet will provide you with most popular names for all years and all nationalities if you need help.

Names may also affect the personality of your character. Would you give a weak sounding name to your strongest character? Would you give the best name you've thought up to a minor character? Think of surnames too. A character might get called by their surname by one character, and something entirely different by another. Calling someone by their surname can alter the mood of a scene. And don't forget nicknames – and the reasons behind them.

Avoid making your character's names sound too similar to each other. Create contrasts to avoid confusion. It's so distracting to be reading a story and having to revert back to see who Amy and Abby were, or Jake and John and so on.

When thinking of a character's first and last names, you might want to contrast them too. Perhaps if you have got a flamboyant first name, let the surname be plainer – and vice versa. But on the other hand, two plain names may sit nicely together and instantly conjure up what that character is like or looks like. Similarly, two flamboyant names together may work well. The choice is entirely yours so give plenty of thought to your characters' names before you christen them.

Step 8: First impressions

As in real life, first impressions count, so aim to create a clear picture when you first introduce a character into your story. I'm not suggesting you write a large chunk of description that would only slow the story down. But try to get across an image of that character for the reader to instantly form a picture and an opinion.

You don't have to tell the reader everything about your character – and certainly not all in one go. But it is important when you first introduce a character that you reveal in some way the most important aspect of their appearance early on. For instance, if you don't reveal that the hero has a long black beard until chapter eight when the heroine gets her engagement ring tangled in it, will completely throw the reader. Provide enough description for the reader to form an accurate picture in their mind rather than an incorrect impression. Then add to this as the story progresses.

By having your character *doing* something as you introduce them will allow you to convey something of their appearance, their personality and their mood. It may even hint at the conflict to come. Showing your character doing something will conjure up a picture for the reader to hang on to. Be aware that the way a character walks and moves says a lot about them – and remember that a character's current mood will affect their mannerisms and conduct.

Think to yourself what this character was doing immediately before you introduce them onto the page.

Characters have backgrounds, and unless your character has just been beamed down from the ether, he or she will have been doing something just before you brought them into your story. Whatever they were doing, thinking and feeling will affect their mood right at that moment.

Step 9: Killing your darlings

We writers are a funny bunch – we slave blood, sweat and tears to create the most realistic, unique, interesting and memorable characters and then, very often, we dispose of them in the most tragic of circumstances.

Even when we're not killing off our darlings, we're putting them through the most traumatic of situations, heaping troubles and burdens on their paper-thin shoulders and pushing them to the limits of endurance. And I thought writers were such nice people!

But it has to be done. If you're going to create a story that will grip the reader, then you must create characters which evoke some sort of emotion in the reader. It doesn't necessarily mean you have to make the reader like your character. It's perfectly fine to make the reader hate the character, or be infuriated with them, or pity them, or any other emotion. So long as the reader feels *something* towards them. The thing you don't want is for the reader not to care.

So, when the time comes in your story where one of your characters must come to a sticky end, what do you need to do, to make sure you write the death scene to the best of your ability?

Here's a few points worth remembering:

- Make sure you've created a character that the reader is interested in. Let them have a backstory, a personality; work to achieve the emotional response in the reader that you intend. So, when they pop their clogs it will mean something to the reader – sadness, glee, satisfaction, shock. It will all depend upon how you've portrayed that character.

- Likewise, if you're getting rid of a villain or an unpleasant character, you will want the reader to feel some satisfaction that they've got what they deserve. Or maybe you'll create a bit of a twist by making the reader feel sorry for them in some way at the end. You could do this by letting your narrative link into some poignant aspect of the character's life as they die, so that it touches the reader in some way – even with the most villainous of characters. Having a little bit of heart or humility or fear in their final seconds can leave a lasting impression on the reader.

- Producing the unexpected is always good. If it's to be a sudden ending, then make it have great impact by your phrasing. Surprise or shock the reader by the turn of events.

- Remember to be tasteful. Don't go overboard with the gore and blood or it might seem gratuitous – there purely for the shock value. You can create a better effect by looking at the

106

emotional side of things rather than the physical.

- It's important to show what effect the death of this character has on other characters, especially your protagonist. If you've done your job right, the reader and your protagonist should be experience similar feelings about this character's demise.

As writers we draw on our own experiences whenever we write, so make sure you have some way of lifting your mood again after writing a particularly draining scene. You probably need to choose your time for writing a harrowing part of your story. And don't forget it's just a story and as writers that's our job as Stephen King says, to *kill your darlings.*

Step 10: Possible problems with characters

Although your characters are not real people, they must give the impression of being real people. However, if they come across as 'wooden' or are rejected by an editor as being unbelievable, then you need to go back to the drawing board.

Firstly, you may not have developed them well enough, or got to know them well enough. Go back to your character sketches and work on them. Write throw-away scenes; interview your characters; look deeper into their backgrounds; make sure their aim or ambition in this story is something worth fighting for.

Here are a few suggestions as to what may have gone wrong, making them seem wooden:

- Characters need to develop throughout the story. Make sure your character has changed in some way by the end of the story. Perhaps they have become a better person, or they have learnt something and grown in some way. Be sure they aren't the same as when the story started.

- Do you really know your characters? Are you forcing the words and actions from them rather than letting them speak and behave naturally? Get to know them better, so they take the lead.

- Are you *telling* the reader what the character is doing, thinking and feeling? *Show* their emotions so that the reader will feel their emotions too. Show through your character's senses all that's going on around them.

- Have you made your characters too good or too bad? Give them some sort of fault or failing to make them human. Similarly, perhaps give your villain some redeeming feature? You don't have to of course. If you're making them despicable, make them totally despicable – that's fun too!

- Are your characters too similar? If so, bring in some contrasts. Make sure it's obvious who's talking by the way each character speaks and what they say.

In a nutshell

- The best way to create characters is to spend time thinking about them and then writing about them.

- Write character descriptions for all your characters.

- Interview your characters. Have a list of personal and random questions. Their answers will surprise you.

- As for your main characters, you need to know every single detail about them. You won't use all this information but it's important that you know it.

- Characters don't just beam down onto the page. They have backgrounds and history. Their past governs the way they are in your story.

- Let the reader know what's going on inside your protagonist's head and heart. Don't just show what the character is doing physically, reveal their feelings too.

- To write effectively the writer needs to be right inside the character's head looking out, seeing the world as they see it.

- Use your character's senses so the reader doesn't just see what they see, but also what the character hears, smells, tastes and feels – physically and emotionally.

- Make your character unique. Ask yourself how you would pick them out in a crowd.

- Give your character their own way of moving or talking or behaving. You could get this across by what others say about them.

- Avoid telling the reader that a character is witty or bad tempered or romantic etc., all these things should become clear through the scenes you write.

- Give your character something they are afraid of. Weave a scenario into the story which demonstrates this.

- Very importantly give your character an aim or a goal that they are trying to achieve in this story.

- Characters interact with one another. They may speak differently or act differently around different people.

- Let your characters talk. Dialogue brings the story to life and shows so much: it shows personality, it moves the story forwards, it provides information for the reader, it sets the mood, it shows what characters think about each other.

- As you have your protagonist with an important aim or goal, then let all your other characters have aims and ambitions, and things they are hoping to achieve. If you have your two main characters with opposing aims, and both as determined to achieve them – then you have the basis for a story.

- Likewise, create characters with very different personalities, backgrounds, beliefs, lifestyles etc.

- Your story must have conflict. Let your character's problems increase as the story moves forward. Let the difficulties become worse until they are almost insurmountable – at the climax of your story. Then through your character's actions, let them succeed or not.

- Allow your character to grow and develop as the story progresses. Don't let your protagonist be the same at the end of the story as they were at the beginning. Let them have learned something from what's gone on.

- If your character doesn't achieve their goal by the end of the story, then let them at least have gained something from the process, and are left with something even better, or some ray of hope.

Exercise 1

Write a detailed character sketch. Be sure to include what this person fears most in life and what their main goal or ambition is in life right at this moment.

Exercise 2

To help you to visualise this character, write a 'throw-away' scene where something is really annoying them. Perhaps they have locked themselves out of the house. Perhaps their car has a flat tyre, or they can't get their own way. How do they behave?

Chapter Ten: Structure, Plotting and Planning

Step 1: The need for structure

Whatever you create, it needs structure. Take a building for example. To start with it needs solid foundations, then comes a sturdy framework around which is attached the fabric of the building. Next comes the décor – the flare of the designer to make that building the best it can be.

Change the metaphor to making a cake. The solid foundation is the cook's knowledge of cookery, of how to follow a recipe, of knowing how ingredients react with one another, of knowing when that cake needs to go in and come out of the oven. The framework is the ingredients and how they combine together. The decoration are the special little touches that make the cake perfect.

It's the same when writing a story. Those solid foundations are your skills as a writer – the knowledge that you've learnt so far. The framework is the many different aspect to a story: characters, setting, viewpoint, plot, conflict, dialogue, narrative, tense, theme, editing and presentation. The décor is your personal style and flair; your descriptions; the depth of the emotion woven into the story; the realism of your characters; it's how effective you are in building tension and atmosphere; it's those unexpected twists and turns in the plot.

Your story isn't just a jumble of words, it's a logical sequence of events that take the reader from the beginning to the end with increasing conflict, tension and interest along the way. Your story structure may be vague or highly detailed, or somewhere in between. Think of it as a guideline that you can follow or veer away from, as you choose.

Don't worry that plotting and structuring will hinder your creative streak or stop the characters from developing. Structure is not carved in stone, you can change things at any time. It is merely a guide, so you don't get lost and helps to avoid writing yourself into a dead end. And best of all, if you can see a vague outline of your story, especially for a book or serial, it's not quite such a daunting prospect to get from A to Z.

Step 2: Planning your story

Take it back to basics – the 3-Act Structure, that is the beginning, the middle and the end. The structure of the plot might be referred to as the story arc. The internet has lots of diagrams that help you think about the shape of your story. You may find them useful – or you may not.

Basically, the story arc is the narrative of your story, showing the development of characters and plot, the rising and falling of character's emotions; the rising and falling of the drama, with everything leading up to the climax of the story – make or break time. Then comes the resolution, the results of what becomes of the characters after the climax, the dénouement, the final act that shows how the character has evolved and grown.

The Beginning

I always find it best to start the story where there is a change to your protagonist's routine, something different is happening in their life. It could be creating a problem or it could be the opposite. You could start with an interesting line of dialogue or some narrative. Whatever those first lines are, make them hook the reader for some reason and make them want to read on. If your beginning is flat and dull don't go thinking that's okay because it really livens up on page ten because your reader may never get that far.

Here's a few examples of opening lines to some of my books:

Without a doubt, Philippe Beaulieu was as magnificent as the pictures he painted. (Champagne Harvest)

'Hexe!' The word rippled around the chamber softly, barely audible, like a breath of wind. (The Bitter End)

The fog came down before midnight. (Kill or Die)

Karbel's yellow eyes sparkled as a shaft of sunlight glanced off the rock. (The Beast)

That opening scene is extremely important. It is where you will interest a reader or editor, or lose them forever. So, make those opening sentences as alluring as possible. Don't try to explain everything at once or even establish the logic behind the words. All can become clear later, once you've got the reader on board.

At the beginning of your story you introduce your main character, you set the scene, and establish the conflict – or at least hint at it. It helps if your protagonist has a goal – something they are desperate to achieve. Make sure this is something worth struggling for – and that applies whether you're writing a book for a toddler, or a hard-nosed detective story. It's just as vital for a two-year-old to find her lost teddy, as it is for the serial killer to be apprehended.

The Middle

At this stage you probably don't have all the events and action sorted in your head. These will come gradually as characters interact with one another. However, there may be key incidents that you know should occur, so you could jot these down as bullet points in your story outline. You may also want to introduce other threads or sub plots into your story.

You will certainly want to make the problems for your protagonist worsen. Incidents will undoubtedly occur to you as your characters develop. Note these points down so you can see the shape of your story. Make sure your character's problems are not resolved too early and the pace of the story is progressing nicely.

I tend to think in scenes, with each scene carrying the story forward and character's problems growing more

116

difficult all the time. One problem or dilemma should lead to another on the journey towards the climax and ultimate conclusion to your story. Basically, give your character a hard time and don't let them get out of trouble too easily.

The End

You may or may not know how your story will end, but you can remind yourself here to tie up all loose ends of your storylines and sub plots – before the climax of the story. The climax of the story should be the most dramatic of scenes, so don't risk diluting the main action by tying up the loose ends at that point.

The climax is where your protagonist wins or loses, achieves his goal or fails. At the crucial black spot of the story, let him or her win or lose through their own actions or decisions – don't bring in the cavalry.

This will be the most intense struggle your character has yet had to face. This is the point where you really want your readers to be rooting for your protagonist. Should they fail, at least let them have learnt something important along the way. Give some ray of hope even to the saddest of endings.

Endings to avoid

- Do not cheat your reader by some surprise twist that is not in the least believable such as a mistake or misunderstanding that could have been sorted out at any time.

- Do not cheat your reader by the introduction of some character or random incident/coincidence that has not been part of your story throughout.

- Do not leave the reader dangling in the air with unanswered questions. Unless of course, that's your intention with a sequel waiting in the wings.

- And please do not let your character suddenly realise it had all been a dream.

Step 3: Writing scene by scene

Personally, I tend to think in scenes rather than chapters or paragraphs or sentences. I try to think what needs to be achieved in that particular scene. It's almost a mini story in every scene – but they need to link together and flow nicely. Take each scene slowly, look to the detail. Bring each scene to life with colour and emotion.

Step 4: Chapter by chapter

If you're writing a book, at the start of each new chapter establish where we are. If your book has more than one viewpoint character, establish whose head we are in. Start and end chapters in a logical place, or at a point where the reader needs to be left dangling. Cliff-hangers make the reader read on. Don't give the reader an opportunity to put the book down. Keep them desperate to know what happens next.

Step 5: Pace

Make it a roller coaster of a ride. Imagine if you were on a fairground ride and it started at the highest, fastest most terrifying moment. The rest of the ride would be something of an anti-climax. So, give your story a dramatic start by all means, but it should not be the most dramatic moment of the whole story.

Be aware too, that while a story needs drama, action and emotional highs and lows, it does not want to be high drama throughout. Give your story a mix of quieter, slower, more relaxed scenes – although never boring and always moving forward, rising gradually to a crescendo.

Step 6: Hold the reader's attention

Keep readers interested not only by the events happening to your characters – and your characters' reaction to events, but in the way you write these incidents. Look to the opposite ends of the scale. For example, high drama incidents hit harder if the scene before is of a slower more relaxed nature. If you are revealing betrayal it will be more acute if the reader has witnessed a previous scene of total trust. If there is a scene of joy it will be more joyful if the reader has coped with the character's sorrow beforehand. If your character is about to step into danger, then the lead up could lull the reader into thinking they were safe.

Step 7: Vary your sentences

Vary their structure, length and even the choice of words, so that it might be read with a feeling of calm, or a feeling of rising tension. Longer words and sentences and descriptive passages will give a more leisurely relaxed sense of being. Short, sharp words and sentences will give the opposite effect. If you can pace your story and mix in unexpected twists and turns, then like a roller coaster ride, your readers will cling on breathlessly to the very end.

In this extract of *The Bitter End*, co written with Robert Tysall, this scene has protagonist Paul and his girlfriend, Sally, calling in at their friend's shop. Note the change of pace, through sentence structure and dialogue. Calm and relaxed at first, then fraught with tension.

The shop was deserted, and Paul checked to see which of his carvings hadn't sold. The clogs and the walking stick were left. Maybe they'd be bought up as Christmas presents, not that it mattered to him one way or the other.

They browsed the shelves for a few moments, waiting for Juliet to appear. Eventually, Sally raised her eyebrows. 'Good job we're trustworthy, we could have made off with the takings and all her stuff by now.'

'Worth giving her a shout?'

Sally nodded and walked to the bottom of the stairs. 'Juliet. Hello. Anyone at home?'

There was no response and frowning, Sally started up the stairs. 'Think I'll just pop up. Hello Juliet, it's me... Sally. I'm coming up.' A moment later she screamed. A shriek of horror. 'Paul. Call an ambulance!'

The operator was asking which service he required.

'Ambulance!' he breathed, taking in the sight that met him.

(No spoilers, so abridged here.)

'Jesus!'

'Sir, are you there? Which service do you require?'

'Ambulance,' he spat out again, before providing the address. 'And the police...Sally, get towels, pad them around the wounds, try and stop the blood. ...'

(Abridged section)

'Ring Owen!' Paul barked. 'Have you got his number?'

'No, no, I haven't. You've got it, haven't you?'

Downstairs, the shop bell tinkled, and Owen called out to Juliet.

Sally gripped his arm. 'Oh my God, Paul!'

Give your story changes in pace by sentence structure and dialogue, and keep the readers reading.

Step 8: Major scenes

While some lesser scenes can simply be told through narrative so that the story moves forward at a good pace, make sure you don't swiftly move through important scenes. They need to be written in all their glory – through a key character's viewpoint, so the reader can experience the event as closely as the character does.

Let readers experience all the emotion and drama; let them hear the actual words being spoken, and not have the scene simply skipped over by a few narrated sentences or they will feel cheated.

Step 9: Plotting

Some writers plot meticulously, others write 'by the seat of their pants' You may have heard the question: are you a plotter or pantzer? There isn't a right or wrong way when it comes to plotting. It's whatever works for you – and you might find you use a different approach to everything you write. You will no doubt find your own way of plotting, but if you're looking for suggestions, here's a few:

- Post-it notes: different colours depicting different moods or characters.

- A story board: sketch out your story.

- A time-line: consider the time covered in your story, and plot hour by hour, day by day, month by month, depending on the time you're covering.

- A numbered list: For example, 1-30. Gauge roughly where major and minor events will come in this list. You will be constantly re-arranging, but that's a good thing.

- If you know the ending, try working backwards logically, scene by scene or chapter by chapter.

Character led stories v plot led stories

Whatever story you're writing, it's all about the characters. If you deliberately plot a story where things happen to that character, it can come across as contrived or forced. Far better if you create really believable characters with personality, background, ideals, dreams, and so on, and allow the story to develop naturally around what they get up to. Your story then becomes character led rather than plot led.

Twists and turns

At a workshop run by *The People's Friend* magazine, the editor talked about the short story as if it were a garden, so I hope she will forgive me for using the same analogy.

If you can look down the garden and see right down to the bottom, then there's no point in walking down the path because you can already see everything. There will be surprises.

However, if that garden is full of twists and turns, and you can't see right down to the end, chances are you'll be curious and interested to know more.

Imagine how pleased you'll be as you come across all kinds of unexpected things as you set out on that journey. You'll keep going, keen to discover more and to learn what is finally at the bottom of that garden. And if the gardener has planted thought, colour and interest all the way through, the journey will be worthwhile.

So, with your stories, you're the gardener, planting out seeds of thought, putting in the colour with the uniqueness of your characters and the setting – and writing narrative that conjures up a picture in the reader's mind. You might know what's at the end of your story, but it's not going to be a straight-forward route in getting there. All sorts of things are going to get in the way of the protagonist before they reach their goal.

It's all about pace. If there are areas in the garden – and the story, that are of less interest but still need to be there, then make the path one that is swift to travel along. Convert that to writing, and you might need to slip in a transition from 'here to there', or from 'now to then'. But there may be other parts of your garden and your story, where you have to stop and take a really good look. In your story, you may need to add more description, or more dialogue to reveal what's happening.

As you know, every story needs conflict – so these might be obstacles in your garden; obstacles that get in the way of your protagonist's aims. These obstacles and the effort needed to overcome them, need to rise in intensity along the way. Your character has to battle to overcome the mounting problems in his way. If it were a garden, you might be crossing streams, battling through brambles, climbing brick walls.

And at the end of your garden – and the story, let there be something there that is worth all the effort, and something feasible but unexpected.

I'm not suggesting you write 'twist in the tail' stories, where the surprise comes at the end – unless you want to. But in every story you write, avoid choosing the easy, expected option for your characters, and the readers. Find your own unique slant even though you might be writing on a common theme.

So how do you create these magical twists and turns?

One way is to begin by free writing. If *you* don't know which way the story is going to go, your reader won't either. Discover together.

Make your characters unconventional in some way, so they don't behave how you might expect them to. Or set your story in an unusual environment – somewhere that's not commonplace. Then, whatever you write, it won't be common knowledge to others.

Perhaps your character works in an unusual trade. It might take additional research, but it will make your story more unique. Or your character's goal is something out of the ordinary. So, why not have a romance blossoming on a trek through the Tianzi mountain? Or a thriller set in the ancient ruins of Hierapolis?

Should you happen to create something that turns out to be obvious, edit your work and change things around. When I was writing my first children's book, *Cry Danger*, I'd practically finished it when I realised that when my villain was revealed there would be no surprises. We knew it was *him* all along. So, after a re-think, I realised it would come as a huge surprise if the villain turned out to be someone else – someone who had seemed so nice and innocent all the way through. Of course, then I had to go back to chapter one and work my way through the book, sowing the seeds, writing in those subtle hints and clues so that when the truth was revealed it was a big surprise to everyone – but totally believable.

In a nutshell

- Know that structure, plotting and planning will not curtail your creativity. It's merely a guideline.

- Don't be afraid to think simply, with a beginning, a middle and an end. Know what needs to go on within each of these three acts.

- Create believable and complex characters, and really get to know them. Avoid the obvious.

- Give your protagonist a goal then put obstacles in their way. Let the problems rise in intensity to the climax of the story.

- Avoid rounding things up too efficiently at the end of a chapter, it gives the reader an opportunity to put your book down. A cliff hanger, or even a poignant sentence can keep them reading.

- Make your story ending surprising but plausible.

- Be aware of the pace of the story, vary sentence structure and mood of different scenes. Hold the reader's attention.

Exercise 1

Take the character that you created in the last exercises, give them a goal or task. Then put obstacles in their way. Let one obstacle cause inner conflict in the character, that is, they are struggling against a personal trait or belief of theirs.

Exercise 2

Make a bullet point list of around 1-30. Each number being where something happens in your story. See if you can create a logical storyline from the beginning, point 1 to the end, point 30.

Chapter Eleven:
Viewpoint, Theme and Grammar.

Step 1: Understanding viewpoint

Viewpoint is through whose eyes, ears, thoughts and emotions the story is told. Be sure that you're writing through the viewpoint of your main character – your protagonist. It is important that the conflict in the story affects this main character personally, so that the reader experiences all their joys and sorrows. If the reader fails to connect with this character they may not read on.

Your story or book may just have one viewpoint character (single viewpoint), or you may decide that you want some scenes or chapters told through the eyes and heart of another important character or characters (multi viewpoints). Either is fine but avoid head-hopping. Don't jump willy-nilly from one character's head to another. Give each viewpoint character their own scene or chapter. In your layout you could indicate a change of viewpoint by adding some extra white space between paragraphs. Make it clear at the start of the new scene that we are now in another character's head.

Short stories tend to be single viewpoint – two at the most. Longer stories and novels could have multi viewpoint characters because the story is more complex. Be selective however, the reader doesn't need to see the story through every character's eyes.

There's also the omniscient viewpoint, which is a kind of God-like approach that's all seeing and all knowing. So, the reader gets to see what every character is thinking and feeling. However, unless you're a very experienced writer – and the story warrants it, writing in this omniscient viewpoint can come across as amateurish. You are aiming for readers to connect with your main character and if you are constantly skipping from one character to another, the reader will not be able to identify with any of the characters and undoubtedly lose interest in the whole thing. If you decide on using everybody's viewpoint, beware that it is the perfect way of making your story nobody's.

Step 2: Theme

To describe what is meant by the 'theme' of the story, I would describe this as being a simple sentence or two that sums up what your story is about. For example, it might be a *rags to riches* theme, or a *love conquers all* theme, or a *revenge is sweet* theme.

However, while other writers might disagree, I'd say that you shouldn't worry too much if you don't know the theme of your story. In my experience, very often the theme doesn't become apparent until you're halfway through or have even finished writing your story.

When you do finally understand the theme, then you can re-work to enhance that theme, making it stronger through the dialogue, narrative and description as you polish and edit.

Step 3: A bit of English grammar

Not wanting this to be a lesson in English Grammar – there are other books that cover the topic far better than I ever could, nevertheless, there are certain aspect of English grammar that writers need to be aware of when writing fiction.

Tense

You need to decide what tense you're writing that particular story in. The tense being the form taken by a verb to indicate the time of action. The major tenses basically are Past, Present and Future. There are many more, but for the purpose of this book, we'll stick to these.

Writing in the **Past Tense** is the most common and versatile tense to use. Here, the character, for example: *walked in, took off his coat and smiled.*

In the **Present Tense**, the character: *walks in, takes off his coat and smiles.*

Should you attempt to write an entire story in the **Future Tense,** that sentence would be along the lines of: *you walk in, take off your coat and smile.*

Although in everyday life we talk a great deal in the **Future Tense**, it doesn't come naturally to write in that tense – apart from dialogue: *"I'll do that, dear." "Shall I drive?"* The future tense refers to a time 'later than now'. As far as I know, there are very few books – if any, written in the future tense. The reason being that the essence of telling a story, is to relate things that are happening or have happened. The whole tradition of storytelling goes back to distant times when our ancestors sat around the campfires telling stories of things that had happened. It's not easy to tell a fictional story about something that hasn't yet happened. But don't let me stop you!

Still on the subject of tenses, we use Past Perfect or the Past Perfect Continuous when we write a flashback: *It had been a beautiful summer...* It's feasible that we might want to use the Future Perfect or Future Perfect Continuous in a scene where your character is daydreaming about an event they hope, or dread will happen – maybe a premonition type of scene.

The great thing about writing is that you can be adventurous. See what works for you. However, don't change the tense in your story unless it's deliberate, and to intentionally create some kind of effect – don't change it because you've made a mistake.

Which Person to write in?

You also need to decide whether you're writing in the 1st Person, 2nd Person or 3rd Person viewpoints.

Writing in the First Person

Some stories work best when written in the 1st Person. Here you write from the perspective of 'I'. However, writing in the 1st Person does not mean it's you, the author, unless it's autobiographical. Otherwise, you need to create a fully rounded fictional protagonist.

Don't think you can get away with not doing this, just because the main character is referred to as *I*, *me* and *my*. There are no short-cuts to be gained by writing in the 1st Person. And exactly as when you're writing in the 3rd Person, the protagonist can't know what's going on in someone else's thoughts, so viewpoint rules still apply. Remember, no head-hopping

Writing in the Second Person

Writing in the second person it's as if you are talking to the reader and you would use the pronouns 'you' or 'yours'. Writing fictional stories in the 2nd Person although possible, is not very popular amongst editors or even readers.

Yet, writing fiction from the 2nd Person perspective could be just as intimate and engaging as if writing from either of the other two perspectives. Maybe more so, if done well, as the author is literally inviting the reader to feel and experience what's going on for themselves.

When writing non-fiction, particularly articles and instructions, writing in the 2nd Person is the perfect way of drawing the reader in to what you're saying. E.g. *Have you ever wondered what it would be like to see your book on the library shelves…*

Writing in the Third Person

This is probably the most popular and easiest to manage. Writing in the 3rd Person is when the protagonist is referred to by name or by the pronouns: he, her, she, he, his, hers, they, theirs, them etc. Exactly the same as if writing through the 1st Person, the story unfolds through their eyes, emotions, actions, thoughts and feelings. You can get just as close emotionally to the character whether you're writing in the 1st or 3rd Person.

Again, the viewpoint rules apply. When writing in the 3rd Person (and 1st Person) you can only know what's going on in this character's head. Your protagonist might surmise or guess what other characters are thinking and feeling but won't know for sure. So, don't go jumping into other character's heads (head hopping).

In a nutshell

- Although these points may seem complicated, it's just basically how people are in real life. We only really know what's going on inside our own mind and body, that's what viewpoint is all about.

- Just as we can't mind-read, neither can our characters.

- Make it clear through a scene change or chapter change if you are changing viewpoint character.

- Don't head hop.

- With tenses, it's far easier to choose to write in the Present Tense or the Past Tense.

- When deciding which Person to write in, the 1st Person (I, me and my) and 3rd Person (he/she, his/her, they, their, by name) are by far the best choices.

Exercise 1

Practice writing in the 1st Person, as if the protagonist is the 'I' / 'Me' character. Write a short scene, perhaps showing the character running for a bus or train or walking through the park. Keep it simple as the emphasis is on getting the viewpoint of the 1st Person correct. You will also need to decide whether you're writing in the Present Tense or Past Tense. See what feels most natural to you.

Exercise 2

Write another scene in the 3rd Person, so the protagonist is referred to by name or he/she, his/her, theirs/they etc. Again, you will need to decide whether to write in the Present Tense or Past Tense. Your choice.

Chapter Twelve:
Dialogue

Step 1: Writing realistic dialogue

The way you write your dialogue can make or break your story. After all your efforts in creating your characters with all their individual traits, personality, appearance, background and so on, it's vital that the way they speak and the things they say, match their personality and mood.

While you want your dialogue to sound like real speech, it actually only gives the impression of real speech. When people are talking in real life, there are lots of y'knows, umms and ahhs, along with repetitions, interruptions and drifting off at a tangent. Real speech in a story would be tedious. The author has to give the impression of real speech with all the boring bits taken out, leaving just the words that are there for a reason.

A few lines of good dialogue can reveal more about character and plot than many pages of narrative. Plus, dialogue brings vitality to a story – it brings your story to life.

Step 2: Reasons for dialogue

Dialogue is there for several reasons:
- To carry the story forward.

- To characterise the speaker and other characters.
- To show the emotional state of the speaker.
- To describe or set the scene or mood.
- To increase the tension and suspense.
- To provide the reader with necessary information.

Make every word of your dialogue count. It is not there to pad out your story. If something is mentioned in dialogue, then it is there for a reason. The reader may not know that reason at that moment, but later in the story it should become clear. If your dialogue is littered with irrelevant, unnecessary facts that come to nothing it can mislead the reader as well as slowing your story down and spoiling it. So, keep it alive and moving forward. Don't allow your characters to get bogged down in a lot of unnecessary banter that does nothing to move the story forward.

Of course, making every word count also applies to your narrative – in fact when you're polishing your story or novel, there should be no superfluous words or long-winded phrases. Every word really should count and be there for a reason.

One piece of advice I picked up years ago, but which has stuck with me, was: if you had to pay 10p for every word you write, you would be meticulous about unnecessary words slipping in.

Be careful not to duplicate. If you've already mentioned something in the narrative, there's no point in bringing it up again in conversation, and vice versa. And while dialogue is great for providing the readers with important information, be careful one character isn't telling another character something they already know, just for the benefit of the reader. Bad example: *"Hello, Sue, I bet you're excited to be marrying Joe today at 3 o'clock at St Jude's and your honeymoon in Paris, particular as you've only known him three weeks."*

Dialogue needs to sound natural with the characters all sounding different from one another.

Step 3: Show don't tell through dialogue

Dialogue is the best way to reveal character, so be sure that in your story you do not simply state that your character is, for example, a man with a quick temper, or a real joker, without writing scenes to show these traits. Similarly, don't just tell the readers about two people being in love, or hating one another. This must be shown through the scenes you write, and the way they speak and behave around one another.

Step 4: Attributions or speech tags

Attribution is the term used to describe who is speaking – *he said*, *she replied, I answered etc.* Some writers feel they need to look for other ways of saying who is speaking and search the thesaurus to find alternative ways of saying 'he said'. In fact, the humble 'he said' is virtually invisible in the context of the story. By using an alternative, it can become conspicuous, drawing attention to itself rather than what is being said. If your story is littered with contrived attributions it will make it appear amateurish. You can vary your character's speeches with equally unobtrusive attributions such as *he replied, he answered, he asked* and similar phrases.

Narrative showing the character doing something either before or after the speech could do away with the need for any speech tags. Also, sometimes the dialogue needs nothing around it, as it's perfectly obvious who is speaking. However, read your work aloud and listen to the euphony and flow of your words. Adjust with the addition or detraction of speech tags or narrative as necessary.

Dialogue is one of the best ways to show the personality of a character and the reader should know who is speaking simply by what is being said and the way it is being spoken. However, be careful not to have a whole section which is nothing but dialogue without narrative or character interaction. The reader does not want to have to count back to see who is talking.

Step 5: Dialect

It can be difficult to write dialogue for characters who come from a region or country with a strong dialect. It's easy to get into a quandary trying to mimic a broad accent, dropping g's and h's and spelling words where the reader has to mentally form the sound in their heads as they read. Not only is this difficult but it also looks awkward on the page. Far better to research and listen to the speech patterns and idioms from the region or slip in a word or phrase that indicates the locality. Be careful this doesn't come across as clichéd, however.

Slang

Certain characters in your stories will undoubtedly need to resort to slang if they are to sound realistic but be careful not to use the latest modern day slang which comes and goes year after year. While it might be the way characters are expressing themselves today, especially younger characters, by the time your book or story comes out, it could be totally outdated – and make your work 'dated' too. Better to stick to the good old fashioned slang words and expressions that have been around for decades.

Additionally, while it's not slang, abbreviated words are important in dialogue. A character saying: *"I have been looking for you."* sounds less natural than: *"I've been looking for you."* Read your dialogue aloud and listen to whether it sounds natural or not.

Four lettered words

For your characters to come across as real people there may be times when you have no alternative but to use a 'four lettered' word. If you feel it is the only thing your character could say under the circumstances, then use it with confidence. However, I would add, that in my mind, this would only apply to adult books, certainly never in children's or YA books.

For adult readership, a swear word may be necessary to create impact and show the character's mood. However, if you have a character who swears continually it will quickly become irritating for the reader. Plus, the impact will be lost. An occasional swear word in a novel can be startling and effective, while a hundred will become tiresome.

Of course, if you're writing fantasy or sci-fi, you can create your own swear words without offending anybody.

Step 6: Let dialogue work for you

Your characters' dialogue doesn't just carry the story forward, it shows the character's mood, emotions and relationships with others. Let dialogue work in heightening the drama of a scene. If even a single word of dialogue isn't there for good reason, then change it for a word or sentence that does add something to the story.

A line of dialogue is the perfect tool for starting off your story as it immediately draws the reader in. As someone is speaking, you're immediately introducing a character. It can reveal personality and how they are feeling right at that moment. It can set the scene and even indicate the conflict and what is at stake. A few good lines of dialogue at the start of a story – or at the opening of any scene can take the place of paragraphs of narrative.

Dialogue is also a perfect choice for ending your story. After all, the reader has stuck with your characters throughout your story, so why not allow one of them to have the final word? I've found that a final line of dialogue can conclude the story perfectly.

Step 7: Punctuation around dialogue

While we looked at punctuation around dialogue in chapter eight, it doesn't hurt to reiterate the rules here. Getting the punctuation correct around dialogue must become second nature to you. So many novice writers get it wrong or fail to be consistent with their layout around dialogue. Remember that *all* the punctuation goes inside the quotation marks. If you're adding a speech tag, you don't capitalise the first letter, even if your final punctuation mark before the closing speech mark is a question mark or exclamation mark. E.g. *"Shall we take the bus?" she asked, glancing at her watch.*

Also note the comma after the attribution. Start a new paragraph for every new character speaking or doing something. Check your settings so that you're not adding extra white space every time you hit the *return* button on your keyboard. Adjust your settings to indent every new paragraph for fiction, unless the magazine guidelines/style says not to.

If you know the publication you're writing for, then check whether they use double or single quotation marks around their dialogue. If you haven't a particular publication in mind, then it's your choice – whatever feels more natural to you. However, in my opinion, I would suggest using double because it's easier for an editor to change those to single if re-formatting your story for publication, rather than the other way around.

It's easy to make mistakes – all those important commas, full stops, quotation marks, exclamation marks, capital letters and uncapped letters. Make sure you have it perfected so that it's second nature to you when you write dialogue.

Don't expect anyone else to put it right for you, it's no one's responsibility but your own. If you don't master the correct way of presenting your dialogue it could spoil your chances with an editor.

So, make it second nature and enjoy your dialogue. Enjoy hearing what your characters have to say and let their dialogue carry your story forward.

Step 8: Having problems with dialogue

If your dialogue just does not sound realistic it may be because you have not created your characters well enough yet. So, spend more time on getting to know them. If you are struggling to find something for them to say, then again it might be because they are not real enough to you yet or the scene has not been set dramatically enough to draw a response and a reaction from them. More groundwork could be needed. Read your dialogue aloud and adjust until it sounds real.

In a nutshell

- Dialogue should sound like real speech but actually it only gives the impression of real speech, with all the boring and unnecessary words taken out.

- Make every word of your dialogue count. It's not there to pad out your story.

- Avoid littering your dialogue with irrelevant, unnecessary facts that come to nothing.

- Avoid duplicating information. If you've already mentioned something in the narrative, there's no point in bringing it up again in conversation, and vice versa.

- Be careful one character isn't telling another character something they already know, just for the benefit of the reader.

- Dialogue needs to sound natural, and let each character find their own way of speaking. Don't allow your characters to all sound the same.

- Attributions/speech tags such as *he said* are fine. If you try too hard over your tags, it draws the reader's attention to it, rather than the dialogue itself.

- Avoid using adverbs too often at the end of

speech tags, E.g. *he said merrily.*

- Combining narrative with dialogue makes the writing flow and enables you to do away with the need for a speech tag.

- Be careful with slang as it can 'date' a story. However, do abbreviate words to make them sound more natural.

- Four lettered words: Think about your audience. Don't ruin your chances of acceptance because of a swear word. In adult fiction, one swear word can add impact whereas constant swearing is boring and irritating to the reader.

- Punctuation around your dialogue is so important. Learn how it should be written. Be consistent and meticulous about it.

- Indent every new paragraph unless instructed not to by the publisher or magazine guidelines. Check also whether to use double or single speech marks.

- A new paragraph should be started every time a new person is speaking or doing something.

- Check your paragraph settings. Make sure you're not adding extra while lines in between paragraphs.

- Make sure all your characters sound different from one another in their speech patterns, vocabulary and tone etc.

Exercise 1

Find a professionally published extract of dialogue and copy it exactly. Take note of where the punctuation goes; take note of where capital letters are used and where they aren't. Check your own work to see how it compares.

Exercise 2

As dialogue practice, write a page or two of mainly dialogue but incorporating narrative, around this scenario: The bridegroom and best man await the arrival of the bride. The bridegroom is getting cold feet, about the wedding.

Chapter Thirteen: Narrative

Step 1: Writing the narrative

The narrative is the voice through which you tell your story. Narrative is what leads the reader smoothly through the story with all its ups and downs, high and low spots, emotions and drama. The narrative is what tells the reader what is going on. For example, it lets the reader know that a Highland warrior is marching down the valley, kilt swinging, his beret tilted to one side. The narrative is what tells the reader that thunderous black clouds are rolling in over the rooftops and that the wind is whipping the leaves into a frenzy.

Your story is a balance of narrative and dialogue. However, there is no set formula to see if you are getting the balance right, this all comes down to your ability to write a story – and that comes with practice.

You might start with narrative, setting the scene and drawing the reader into this new world. Or you might start with dialogue and then narrate the next few paragraphs to define who and where your characters are and what is going on. Narrative, like dialogue, advances your story. Narration works hand in hand with viewpoint, so that the writer can merge a descriptive passage smoothly into the key character's thoughts and actions.

The setting for your story is obviously very important. And the settings will change from scene to scene. The narrative voice will portray these settings, letting the reader in on this world, which so far is a product of your imagination. Your narration as you tell the story must engage and interest the reader. It must describe scenes and characters and stir the emotions of the reader.

Through narrative you set the scene, you describe what is going on, and you move the story forward. You show the reader what you can see in your mind. You have to paint the picture and open up this imaginary world where these imaginary people are battling with the many obstacles littering their path. But be careful not to sit back in your typist's chair as you, the author, describe this imaginary scene through *your* eyes. Stick closely to your viewpoint character and let the narrative go hand in hand with their emotions.

Your own style of writing narrative will reveal itself the more you write. It is down to you to polish that style until you create scenes which are vivid, yet not too flowery. Too much and you will be writing 'purple passages' which are gushing with sentiment. Too little and your story could be dull.

There is a very fine line however in the narration of the story and the author talking – giving the reader that extra bit of information that suddenly jars them from the world of make believe and allows them to hear the author's voice. You as author, should stay well hidden – have faith and trust in your characters. If the author goes beyond the narration and pops in their own thoughts, opinions, or additional information, it instantly jolts the reader from this fictional world and reminds them that the author is still there, pulling the strings. The reader does not want that. This story is between them and the characters, the author must remain out of sight.

Find your narrative voice and let that voice speak throughout the story, linking the passages of dialogue, keeping the whole thing flowing smoothly. If you are tempted to add in some piece of random information for good measure, or to start preaching or stating an opinion, then hit the delete key and find some natural way for your characters to pass this information on, either through their actions, their thoughts or through their dialogue.

When writing description avoid writing the obvious. Pick on the most poignant aspect of a person, place or thing. Tell the reader something they didn't know. Find your own unique ways of showing and describing. Don't let descriptions slow the story down.

You might want to get across what your hero or heroine looks like. You may have spent hours researching the outfits they are wearing. But to write paragraphs of description can have the reader impatient to know what these two characters are actually going to say to one another. So, blend your descriptions with movement of the characters so the story is continually moving forward, and at the same time supplying the reader with all the necessary imagery in their mind's eye.

Step 2: Atmosphere and mood.

So, you have planned your story carefully, you know your characters so well they are practically your best friends, and it is all jogging along nicely. The thing is you don't want your story to jog nicely along, you want it to bring tears to your reader's eyes, or make them laugh out loud, or make them so involved they miss their bus stop, or read long into the night even though they know they will struggle to get up in the morning.

To keep the reader gripped and hanging on to your every word, you need to bring in changes to the pace and the atmosphere of your story. Avoid keeping it on one straight level, let moods darken; let the atmosphere become more tense; let heartbeats quicken; bring the reader in even closer to what's happening to your character.

Before you can do this, you need to create a character who the reader cares about. And the way you get a reader to care, is to let the reader in on your character, let the reader understand what's going on in that character's mind – reveal their inner worries and concerns; show that they are human by the things they do, say, think and feel. Strive to make the reader identify with them in some way.

Once you've hooked the reader in that way, when things become more difficult, or the mood darkens, then the reader will feel the tension and keep turning those pages.

Changing the atmosphere is down to your planning – you may have decided earlier that at a particular point in your story, something dramatic will happen; or that particular scene might just creep up on you unawares as you write. Whichever way it happens, when you have a scene that requires some change in atmosphere or mood, then work your magic on it to make it really effective.

I'm a firm believer in the calm before the storm. If the scene just before the dramatic moment is a complete opposite, then the contrast of calm/frantic, relaxed/tense, works really well. Then, once you get into the scene where tension rises, you keep on going, adding layer after layer of drama as the character's situation becomes more and more precarious.

So, these layers, what exactly do they comprise of?

- Make the character's senses heighten. Let them become more aware of things around them, smells, sounds, tastes, things they see are now more threatening.

- It's more effective to show all this through the character's perspective, rather than you simply narrating what's going on around the character.

- Draw the reader closer so they experience everything that the character experiences.

- Tighten those sentences.

- Deliberately repeat a word to empathise a point.

- Physical changes to surroundings e.g. weather, light/dark, silence/noise, movement/stillness etc.

- Dialogue. What your character(s) say and how they say it.

Let your characters talk to each other

As you know, characters need to communicate with each other. Tension, conflict, anger, hatred, love, can all develop through characters talking to one another. Characters can reveal they are afraid or anxious or show the drama rising through their speech and what they say. Staccato dialogue shows their breathlessness. Maybe they don't have time to speak at length, even the narration should come across in that same short sharp manner. Dialogue that is interrupted, or the speaker stops abruptly fearing they have said too much can all help to increase the tension; the occasional ellipsis can work wonders, if used sparingly.

Here's a few examples of showing mood change through dialogue:

"Another coffee, dear?"
"Don't mind if..." Jane stopped in mid-sentence. Her nose wrinkled. "What's that smell?"

Another example:

"Pete, if this is your idea of a joke. If you've set me up..."
He laughed. "Course I haven't..."
His voice trailed away.
"What?" Sue demanded. "What? Speak to me. You're scaring me now."
In a voice no more than a whisper he said, "What do you think that is, standing over there?"

Even the way one character addresses another can indicate the change in mood. Imagine if Mary normally called her husband, Joe. What kind of mood do these alternatives suggest?

"Joseph, I'm talking to you!"
"Oh, Joey... have you got a moment?"

Step 3: Location

Be imaginative when setting the scene. Avoid the obvious or find something different or unusual about a normal setting. There's no point in wasting words to describe something everyone knows about. Pick out an element that makes it different and describe that instead.

Look for contrasts to the 'norm' for the locations in your stories. For example, the setting for a ghost story might well be in a ramshackle old house in the middle of nowhere, but it could be equally as atmospheric if the ghost haunts somewhere as ordinary as an office, a library, a hospital ward, a school sports hall.

Why not make your location in acute contrast to the emotional theme, for example love blossoming amidst the hostilities of a war or a riot; or murder at a joyful family celebration.

As you narrate and describe a place, remember it's not just what can be seen, but the sounds and smells of that place too. Keep your viewpoint character close as you describe a setting. Wherever possible, let it be how the character perceives it – and that will be governed by their mood at that moment.

Step 4: Changeable weather

We all complain about the weather, but writers can actually do something about it – and should. The weather can enhance a scene and add massively to the mood and atmosphere. Take note of how so many writers engage the might of Mother Nature to make a scene more dramatic. Hurricanes, storms, thunder and lightning, dense fog, a blinding blizzard. The list goes on.

The weather can make all the difference to a scene. A wild and stormy night for example, can make everything seem even more dramatic and chaotic. Imagine a storm raging, thunder exploding and lightning crackling, rain lashing down, and your characters are having to shout to each other to be heard. Or imagine the blistering heat of the Sahara Desert and your character trying to trek across the burning sands as hot grit is whipped into their eyes. Imagine your character walking home from school in a thick fog where they can't see a hand in front of their face. Or wading through a heavy fall of snow which has stopped the traffic and is up to their knees as they trudge exhausted on. The weather can help you create the perfect mood for every scene you write.

A sudden cold breeze...
A black cloud passed over the sun...
The moon slunk behind a cloud...
Explosions of lightning zig-zagged across the sky...
A torrent of rain blinded her...

The next time you encounter some intense weather, take careful note – make notes. Look at how the clouds roll in; see if you can taste and smell the fog, try and describe in words that smell and taste – be aware of how it disorientates you; see the different shades of sky and clouds during a thunder storm; look at the colours of sunsets and daybreaks. Try and find the words that will describe these scenes and do them justice. Whenever you personally are drenched in a cloudburst, or freezing in a snowstorm, write up those emotions and sensations as soon as you can – no doubt they will come in useful. (Get warm and dry first though.)

Step 5: Show don't tell

You will have heard that phrase many times, so be sure you are acting upon it. Your story needs to engage the emotions. It's no use simply saying that a character was feeling this way or that way; it's no good saying they were feeling angry or feeling sad. It's through the character's actions, reactions, words and thoughts that you need to *show* them being angry or being sad – or any one of the many emotions people feel: misery, jealousy, grief, joy, sympathy, love, hate and so on.

There's a fine line between showing and telling. You show what's going on through the story narrative. It ends up as 'telling' when the narrative takes it a step too far; when the author chips in and blatantly tells the reader something they feel they need to know. It's when you're offering too much information.

If it's that important, find some way of letting the characters impart this to the reader. The author should have the confidence in their characters to do so, and not feel the reader won't understand unless they add their two-pennyworth. Words to watch out for that might indicate you're about to *tell*, could include: *because, for* and *as*.

Step 6: Using all your senses

To bring a scene to life and allow the reader to experience the events in all their glory, write using all your senses – taste, touch, smell, sound, sight – and not forgetting your sixth sense, that ability to just 'know' something.

Sight

Readers know what everyday objects look like, so pick out the unusual aspect or angle, or focus on something that has specific meaning to the character, perhaps something that brings back memories or affects their emotions in some way. To increase suspense, why not have normal everyday things suddenly appearing wrong. If you've seen the film 'Sleeping with the Enemy' you'll remember the chilling effect those neatly stacked tins and folded towels created.

Little things associated with an unpleasant character can increase tension. Perhaps your villain smoked cigarettes, so the stub of one left on the heroine's doorstep might heighten her fear. The sight of a footprint or a large paw print in the soft earth might add tension; or the sight of something just disappearing out of sight; or the glimpse of a shadow; or the glare of car headlights. Whatever you choose to mention in your narrative, let it be there for a reason.

Sound

Bring a scene to life by allowing your reader to hear the sounds that your character can hear. Think of the background noises whether your characters are in a factory, a supermarket, on a beach, in an aircraft or wherever. If there is a sound that is out of place in that situation, be sure to let the reader hear that. Let us hear the tone of someone's voice when they speak and the way that is modulated depending who they are talking to. When increasing tension, emotion and atmosphere, draw attention to sounds that may not have been noticed before. A quiet room can become even quieter if you can hear the ticking of a clock, or the soft popping of a gas fire, or the sound of their own breathing. You can heighten the suspense in a story by writing in the softest sounds – a whisper, a creak. The softest sounds are often the most affective.

Smell

We have all experienced how certain smells conjure up different memories and feelings. A certain smell can whisk you back decades. Freshly baked bread, a particular perfume or aftershave, a fish and chip shop, a sea breeze, an oily garage, bacon and eggs cooking, lilies, roses, newly mown grass, freshly ground coffee. Use your sense of smell in your writing to bring a scene to life. And when you want to emphasise the mood even more strongly, focus your character's attention on the smell of something specific and meaningful.

Taste

Your characters may taste lots of good and bad things throughout your story, but again use the ploy cleverly when you really want to arouse the emotions. Let them taste things other than food. How about the taste of their lover's lips against theirs? Or taste rain on their tongue; or snowflakes or fog. At the other end of the scale, let them taste fear, let it be so tangible that they can taste it. Perhaps they are so sickened that they taste the bile burning in their throats. What if they are so wracked with misery that their favourite food tastes like wood shavings and sticks in their throat? As people know what certain things taste like, be selective in what you choose to write about – pick out the more unusual things to taste, or when things taste wrong for some reason.

Touch

This sense can portray so much. People in love want to touch each other constantly, to be close, holding hands, caressing, cuddling. Parents hug their children; people stroke their pets; strangers do not touch and if they do, there is embarrassment and apologies for invading the other person's space. Acquaintances might shake hands. We touch and feel so many things, the silky fabric of a ball gown; the smooth surface of an expensive piece of furniture or ornament; we might touch a leather coat to feel its softness and suppleness. Let your reader feel your character's world through the sensation of touch.

The sixth sense

Sense is all about awareness, of perception and recognition. That sixth sense is our extra sensory perception, which some people have more than others. It's a feeling of knowing something when really there's no evidence to support it. I'm a big believer in allowing my character to have that sixth sense – not in a constant mystical way, but just occasionally it can work wonders, when your character just senses that something is going to happen. *Something bad was coming their way...* Often it works a treat if you're aiming to send a shiver down the reader's spine.

Step 7: Handling transitions

Your characters and your readers often have to move from one place to another; from one time to another; or from one emotion to another. The device for moving smoothly from scene to scene is called a transition.

A transition might only be a few words, or it could be a number of sentences. You might need a transition to bridge a highly dramatic scene when the character needs time to think before moving on to a scene with a totally different atmosphere. Your one or two sentences can move your story on an hour, a week, a year; or from the highlands of Scotland to a beach in the Bahamas.

In time transitions, you could use simple phrases, such as:
- The following morning…
- That evening…
- A week later…
- At the end of the week…

Here are a few transitions where there is a change of scene:
- Some miles away…
- In the train on the way back…
- Thick snow had fallen overnight…
- The drive to the hospital was agonising...

A transition should be simple and swift with the objective of getting from *here* to *there* quickly and smoothly, so that you can get on with the story.

Step 8: Flashbacks

If it is necessary to show something that happened in the character's past, which motivates and affects the characters actions, emotions and attitude towards something currently in your story, this is called a flashback. Note that I've said *if it's necessary.* Avoid putting in flashbacks just for the sake of them. They are there for a purpose, be selective of where and why you write in a flashback, and make sure the scene from the past that you choose, reflects why the character is the way they are today.

To handle a flashback so it does not confuse the reader or bring the present action to a grinding halt, the author needs to write it with care. It does not have to come in one big scene, it can be effective to weave fragments of flashbacks into the action and dialogue of your story, so the reader glimpses bits of a tantalising past.

If your flashback needs to be a complete scene or a number of scenes, then find a way of framing this section between the present action, both before and afterwards, so there is no doubt in the reader's mind when they are leaving the present to go into the past, and when they are leaving the past to return to the present.

A change in the tense is important. If you're writing in the past tense, when the viewpoint character is reminded of something that sets their thought drifting back, change the past tense to the past perfect: *had been.* Continue to use that *'had'* for perhaps another sentence or two, to establish that we're now in a flashback. Then phase the *'hads'* out and write normally. When the flashback scene is coming to an end, you could slip a *'had'* back in again, reminding the reader it had been a flashback, and bring the story back to the present. Or putting in the word *'now'* can establish we're back.

Here's an (abridged) example of a flashback scene taken from my award-winning children's book, *The Beast.*

Karbel (the beast) is a ghost and he's suddenly remembering the day he died – at the hands of the boy he is now looking at.

It was him!

Karbel's yellow eyes became slits of hatred.

In a flash, Karbel recalled that fateful day. His final day. A day which could never be erased from his memory.

It <u>had been</u> a long, bitter winter, millennia ago. Snow was up to his belly and he was hungry. In the valley there <u>had been</u> a human settlement which normally Karbel kept well away from, but that winter hunger forced him to venture near. It would be easy picking to snatch a human's baby offspring.

Hunger drove him into the settlement…

(the rest of the scene is written in normal past tense up to the point of the boy saving his baby sister and killing the beast)

…the boy thrust the dagger clean into the beast's heart. Karbel's spirit was ejected violently from his mortal body and he witnessed his own lifeless, bleeding carcass drop into the snow.

The face of the boy without fear was etched into his

soul. And <u>now,</u> as Karbel looked down into the valley he saw that same face. Recognised that same fearless spirit...

And on we go with the story. The flashback scene is neatly 'sandwiched', and the flashback was vital as there was no other way to show that Karbel believes the boy killed him and is now back to take his soul. And that leads to the whole book's premise of Karbel going after the boy.

So, if you need to write a flashback, be bold about it. Sandwich it neatly between the point in the story when the character is reacting to something from their past. Change the tense, use those *'had beens'* or similar phrasing. Show what happened, and then get back to the story, neatly and confidently.

An alternative, if your flashback is a short scene, it could be revealed through dialogue. Simply have two characters talking and one telling the other about a past event.

If the flashback scene involves characters from the past in conversation, be very careful that the whole thing does not get confused.

And if you find you are writing most of your story as a flashback, then possibly you have started your story in the wrong place at the wrong time. A re-think might be necessary. In short stories however, this can work effectively, especially if you are looking for a twist in the tail ending. As when you return to the present towards the end of your story, you can reveal something surprising yet believable.

Step 9: Keep the reader reading

Whether you're writing a short story or a novel the outcome is the same – you want the reader to be so captivated by your words they can't put your story down until they've reached the very end. So, keeping hold of the reader's interest is something that needs to be worked on. And there are lots of little ploys that can be woven into your fiction that help to do just that.

Firstly however, you must have a good story, believable characters, realistic dialogue, a gripping flawless plot, written without superfluous words and continually moving forward with vocabulary that's a pleasure to read. And then you can start to be a bit crafty!

When I've found a good book that keeps me reading, it's often because there's no let up from the action, the protagonist hasn't resolved their troubles. Before one problem is solved another is just beginning. Be sure to have things happening in your story, don't allow it to become stale or slow.

Be guided by your own judgement. If a section you're writing feels even slightly long winded or tedious to you, then look to shorten it, either in content or in the sentence structure. Or consider whether it's even necessary.

Of course, you don't want every sentence and scene to be high drama, but when the action isn't so dramatic or intense, then feed the reader with tasty little morsels or hints of the drama to come. You can do this either through narrative or dialogue. For example, this snippet of dialogue foretells trouble: *"We can't go there, haven't you heard the legend?"*

Or a little narrative to sow the seed of more drama to come: *She put the creaking of upstairs floorboards down to the house settling for the night.*

The occasional repetition of a word or a poignant phrase can work well to keep the reader on board. A word or phrase they've heard before in the story, but then said in a different context can be effective.

In *The Beast*, when the strange old Scotsman tells Grant and Amanda to *"Beware the Beastie"* they find it hilarious. But later in the story, when they sense something stalking them, the old man's words, *"Beware the Beastie"* take on a far more sinister meaning.

And look at punctuation and sentence length. Short punchy sentences can give a breathless effect to a scene. Likewise, with dialogue, you can really create drama and mood through your characters' conversations.

Still with *The Beast*, the valley where Grant and Amada are camping is reputed to be haunted and early one morning:

"You must be able to hear it. Listen, Grant. It's coming from the valley."

"What is? I can't hear a thing."

Amanda swung round to face him, her frown heavy over her eyes. "Are you deaf or what? There are people coming this way...I can hear an enormous crowd of people heading right toward us. And horses, can't you hear the hoof beats? Can't you feel the vibrations through the ground?"

Grant slowly shook his head. "Manda, it's as silent as the grave out here."

"Shouting! They're shouting now!" She gripped his arm. "And screaming." Her voice rose. "Can't you hear those screams, those horrible shrieks? Like...like people killing each other."

Grant put his arm around her. "We'd better go and get Mum."

"What's happening, Grant? What's happening to me?"

It might be a cliché but remembering *the calm before storm* can certainly work when pacing your story. When you have a tense scene about to happen, ensure that the scene before is the complete opposite. Trust/betrayal; love/hate; tranquillity/chaos etc. So, when the drama happens it has more impact because of what's just gone on.

Another little ploy when you want to 'up' the tempo of your story, is to create a change – perhaps in the environment your character finds themselves in; or a change in the weather; or a change in the atmosphere in

165

some way. Have something happening which triggers that switch.

Step 10: Cliff-hangers

One sure way of increasing the tension and the dramatic high spot is by having cliff-hangers. Plan your scenes so that the most dramatic spot can come at a point where you can break off for a new chapter. Build each scene up to its most exciting point – then stop. Perhaps your character is left in a tricky position emotionally or physically.

A new chapter may provide fresh momentum, or you may keep your reader hanging on in suspense while you deal with another thread of your story. Maybe that too can be brought to boiling point. You could be like a juggler spinning plates, precarious yet balanced so perfectly with you in control.

Step 11: Read aloud

And finally, if you want the readers to keep reading, then read your work yourself – out loud. By doing so, you'll hear the euphony of your sentences and phrasing. You'll get a good ear for how it should sound and how it does sound. Awkward sentences may only need a word taken out or putting in, or a slight alteration of the punctuation. Read aloud and only pause where you've indicated a pause with a punctuation mark. The smallest little tweak to a sentence can make all the difference.

So, go through your story and see if by re-phrasing certain sections you can add to the atmosphere or build tension. See if you can create little ploys of your own – barely noticeable things which only register in the reader's subconscious. Occasional words in italics for example; or the repetition of a word or sentence that turns it into something poignant or sinister. Could you subtly hint that disaster is soon to befall the character? Could there be a recurring thought, word or phrase that jabs at your character when things are getting tricky? Experiment with your writing and see what works and what doesn't.

Step 12: Making sense of it all

When planning your stories, consider what sort of emotion you are trying to get your readers to feel. For example, in a thriller or crime story you might want to generate a foreboding mood through your writing. This might be achieved by dropping in little hints of troubles to come; or creating darker scenes through your narrative. Dialogue could include a character's worries and concerns; you might pile on the layers of difficulties to add to that overall sense of foreboding through your description, narrative and dialogue.

The same applies if you're trying to create a sense of intrigue and mystery. Let everything you write go towards that mood and atmosphere. Or perhaps you're writing about the grandeur of something, a royal palace, a sumptuous banquet, so you want to create a sense of occasion. Again, build up the atmosphere through description, using all the senses.

Maybe you're trying to write something humorous. You'll definitely be hoping your readers will have a sense of humour and will see the funny side of what your characters are saying and doing. You'll no doubt find that the characters themselves aren't deliberately trying to be funny. The humour often happens through their tragic circumstances, as things go wrong for them.

So, think carefully about the mood and atmosphere in your scenes, know what sort of 'sense' you're trying to get across to readers. Keep that in focus as you write your stories.

Common sense

Unless you're writing about a Frank Spencer or Homer Simpson type of character, then your characters should be blessed with a bit of common sense. So that in any given situation, they would use their common sense. And this is worth remembering if you're not going to irritate your reader. For example, your character might be facing some sort of emotional or physical conflict that could be easily sorted if they just used their common sense.

Try not to let your plot become contrived – if a character's difficulties could all be overcome if they'd just used their common sense. For example, all would have been sorted if they'd spoken to Uncle George, or opened the letter, or said they were sorry etc. It's so annoying for the reader when the character doesn't do the obvious.

If it would ruin your plot for them not to act in the most obvious way, then be sure you have a very good reason for them not to have acted as any normal person would. Otherwise readers and editors with be groaning with frustration. Look at your plot and make sure your characters do the obvious. It might mean you thinking a lot harder about the conflict facing them, and their situation.

Sensing when it's right

As writers, we have to use our senses too, especially when trying to work out whether we've got a piece of writing right, or whether there's something wrong with it. Far better to sense that it's not right and then to work on improving it, rather than thinking it's great – when it's not.

So how do you do that? I can only say that it comes with practice and with learning. Writing is a craft that you can learn. If you don't bother learning the rules of grammar, punctuation, viewpoint, the tenses, adverbs, dialogue etc., then you won't be able to see your mistakes. Additionally, it's so important to read. You learn by reading and seeing how other writers create their magic.

But even if you've done all that, you still need to develop a sense of knowing whether your work is finally as good as you can get it – or not. This comes with edits. You need to go over and over your work, tweaking, re-arranging, re-phrasing, reading it aloud, listening to the euphony of every sentence, listening for repetitions.

Look out for bad writing habits. Know when something jars. Have a keen ear and listen to anything that doesn't sit quite right.

If you're looking to create a tear-jerking scene, it should bring tears to your eyes. If you're creating a dramatic scene, then you should feel anxious as you read it. If you're creating a humorous scene, it should at least bring a smile to your face, no matter how many times you go over it.

Be critical of your own work, but not to the extent that you're never happy with it, or you lose confidence in your abilities as a writer. Develop that sense of knowing when something isn't right, but also develop the sense to know when it's well written. Learn to trust your own senses.

In a nutshell

- Always aim to keep the reader reading. Don't make it easy for them to put your book down, or to put your short story aside before finishing it.

- Don't let there be a let up from the action. When one trouble is over another one is just beginning.

- When the action isn't so dramatic or intense, consider using a transition to move the story forward. Also, feed the reader with tasty little morsels or hints of the drama to come.

- Plot and plan your story scene-by-scene, or by chapters so action and/or emotion rises to a crescendo at the end of that scene/chapter. Stop at a point where the reader is desperate to know what's coming next.

- Don't be afraid to use cliff-hangers. Let your protagonist be in some sort of predicament – emotionally, physically or both.

- If you have more than one viewpoint character, make them as interesting as each other.

- If a section is feeling even slightly long winded or tedious to you, shorten it, either in content or in the sentence structure. Or consider whether it's even necessary. Make every word count.

- When describing people and places and things, pick out the most poignant aspects. Always tell the reader something they didn't know.

- Create characters that the reader will be interested in.

- Use good dialogue to move the story forward. Let characters say how they are feeling.

- Hint at troubles to come though the narrative and the dialogue.

- Adjust punctuation. You can create tension through your punctuation. Add a more breathless feel to a section by deliberately shortening the sentences.

- Occasionally highlight poignant words, phrases or thoughts in italics.

- Always use the senses. Let the reader see, hear, feel, smell, touch and taste everything the character experiences.

- When you want to 'up' the tempo of your story, let there be a deliberate switch, something happening in the story that changes everything.

- Plan scenes to give a 'calm before the storm' type of feel.

- Make good use of the weather and environment to add drama and atmosphere.

- Show don't tell: Don't say a character is afraid/happy/excited etc, show it by how they behave and what they say, do and think.

- Read aloud. You may find that adjusting the punctuation and re-phrasing may turn something mundane into something dramatic.

Exercise 1

Write two consecutive scenes which show a contrast in the character's moods or the atmosphere of the scene. For example, a scene where everything is going right followed by a scene where it is all going horribly wrong. Let the weather have an impact on how your character is feeling and behaving.

Exercise 2

As an exercise think of an object. Now describe it using the relevant senses i.e. what you might see when looking at it; what sounds it might make; what it tastes like; what it feels like; what it smells like. Ask a friend or relative to try and guess what you have described. Repeat the exercise until you are bored (or your friend is).

Chapter Fourteen:
Editing and Re-writing

Step 1: Editing your work

Difficult though it may be to write your story or novel in the first place, the editing and re-writing of it is just as necessary – if not more so. Never be satisfied with you first, second or even third drafts. Editing is what can turn good writing into great writing. That in turn can make the difference between an acceptance letter and a rejection slip. So be prepared to re-write your work time and again, honing and polishing until it shines.

However, knowing how to edit and improve your writing is something of a skill in itself. Unless you know what you are looking for, you may struggle to improve upon your initial writing. Or you might cut away too much and totally ruin your work. So, it's a good idea to make a copy of your story to work on and keep your original draft intact. If nothing else, you can compare your early draft to your honed and polished story. But on the other hand, if you make radical changes which you later regret, you still have your original draft to return to.

All writers have their own approach to writing and editing. Perhaps you have been re-writing and polishing as you have gone along. Even so, you will need to look again at your finished work, to double check that it is the very best you can do. Other writers prefer to just crack on with their story and not look back until it is finished.

Only then do they start looking at how to edit and improve it. There is no right or wrong way. It is entirely up to you. However, be sure that you do edit, polish and re-write. I doubt there is a writer born who can write something word-perfect at the very first attempt.

Step 2: How to edit your story

After slaving away for weeks, months or even years, you finally type *The End.* Undoubtedly, you will breathe a huge sigh of relief, and possibly that relief will be tinged with sadness that your involvement with your characters has come to an end. But if you think your next step is to send it winging its way to the nearest publisher, think again. Do that and you can be sure it will come winging its way home even faster. Certainly, congratulate yourself on completing your story, whether it is a short story or a full-blown novel, it is quite an achievement and you should be proud of yourself. But there's still work to be done.

Step 3: Let it rest

Put your story aside for a while. You will be too close and too closely involved to look impartially at it straight away. So, let it rest for a while, even if only for a few days. Some writers believe in letting their work rest for months before returning to it with that critical eye.

Of course, you will have your own way of editing, but here is one suggestion. After a decent break from it, read it from start to finish, with a notebook and pen to hand to jot down anything that jars, or fails to make sense, or is badly written. Anything in fact that needs looking at. Be prepared to make changes and re-write sections if necessary. Careful and meticulous editing could make all the difference between getting your story accepted or rejected. After spending so much time already on it, you owe it to yourself to give it the best chance possible.

Step 4: What is it all about?

Looking at your story with fresh eyes, look out for holes in the plot, unexplained events, inconsistencies, and loose ends not tied up. Ask yourself whether you believe in your story. Does the plot feel contrived? Have the characters led the way or have you as author pulled all the strings? You *must* believe in your story, your characters and this whole make-believe world that you have created. Even fantasy needs to be utterly believable. If *you* don't believe in it, then no one else will either. If you find that you do not completely believe in your story, then ask yourself why not. What would make it more realistic to you? Then act upon this.

Check if you have got into any bad writing habits such as using the word '*just*' too often or '*starting*' or '*that*' or other words adding nothing to the content.

E.g. She had just sat down when the phone rang.
Just then…
He started towards the door…
She started to smile…

There was nothing that she could do about it…

Step 5: Look at your characters

Your characters are at the heart of your story, it would be nothing without them. Are they believable or are they wooden? Have you brought them to life through movement, action, reaction, speech and emotion? Have *you* controlled their every thought, word and deed or somewhere along the line have they taken over and surprised you with the things they have said and done? Ideally, that is what you should be expecting to find, that your characters have become so real, they have brought their role to life and you as the author have given them the leeway to carry on.

Have you described them well enough for the reader to visualise them in their own mind? Is their back story strong enough to make them feel like real people? Look to see if your key character has changed in some way from how they were at the start of the story. Have they learned something, or moved on in some way? It is important that they are not the same at the end of the story as at the beginning. Let your characters grow.

Step 6: Listen to the dialogue

As you know, dialogue should give the impression of real speech – that is real speech with all the boring bits taken out. Check that you have not left any boring bits in. Make sure that every word of dialogue has earned the right to be there. Don't pad your story with irrelevant speech that adds nothing to the story. Cut out laborious dialogue if the reader already knows that information via the narrative. Your dialogue should always be adding something new and relevant to your story. Also, look at your speech tags. Could you cut back on the '*he saids?*'

Step 7: Lacking emotion and atmosphere?

Are you caught up with the emotions of your characters? If not, why not? Maybe their problems are not taxing enough – in which case a major re-think could be needed. Maybe you have not described scenes well enough. Remember to bring all the senses into play. Evoking an emotion in the reader is so important. You want the reader to care about your characters. They need to be emotionally involved in your story.

Step 8: Look at the narrative

Look and listen to the voice of your story – the narration. Let it be in line with the story itself and its characters. Let the tone of the narrative be at one with the rest of the story. A love story does not require a cynical narrative; a thriller will not want a jovial approach. Keep the viewpoint of your main character close at hand when the narrative is written so that they go hand in hand. Be sure it's not you, the author who is narrating this story; get inside the head of the protagonist as you write.

Is there too much narrative? Have you narrated major scenes that should have been enacted 'live' before the reader's eyes to evoke their emotion? Do you need to re-write certain scenes to bring them to life? Have you painted a clear picture of the world these characters live in? Watch out for sentences that tell instead of show. If there is 'too much information' then start deleting. Similarly, if there are purple passages, i.e. sections which slow the story down and are only there to show what a brilliant writer you are – then hit the delete key. Could you rephrase to make sentences more succinct? Are there superfluous words that could be cut out?

Step 9: Viewpoint

Do we see the story unfolding through the eyes and heart of the protagonist? Be sure you have not flitted in and out of the heads of other characters unintentionally. It's too easy to accidentally show what another character is thinking or feeling who isn't the viewpoint character. Watch out for slips like this. Similarly, with the tenses – have you been consistent? Go through your story and make the changes necessary – or make a note of sections that need more work so you can return to re-write them after you have given them more thought.

Step 10: Go back to basics

- Look for spelling mistakes and grammatical errors.

- Look at the presentation. Is it double spaced, is each paragraph indented or as your market requires?

- Check the punctuation around dialogue. Have you got it perfect – consistently perfect?

- Look for exclamation marks, and if you find any anywhere except in your dialogue – short bursts of dialogue preferably, delete them.

- Have you started a new paragraph with each character change – dialogue or action?

- Look out for excessive adjectives and adverbs.

In a nutshell

- If you want to write for publication re-write and re-write.

- Never be satisfied with your first draft. Authors re-write constantly.

- Read your work out loud – or get someone to read it to you. Listen out for anything that sounds clumsy and doesn't flow.

- Does your work start with a sentence that really hooks the reader? Does it make you want to read on? Are your main characters doing something of interest when you first introduce them?

- Is it clear whose viewpoint the story is being told through? Avoid 'head-hopping'. Stick to your protagonist's viewpoint. Or start a new chapter or at least a scene break before changing viewpoint character. The omniscient viewpoint of seeing and hearing all, leads to a weaker story.

- Is your main character faced with difficulties that they will struggle to overcome? If there's no conflict in your story, then there's no story.

- Is every word of your characters' dialogue necessary? Does it have a reason for being there? Dialogue should give the impression of real speech with all the boring bits taken out.

- Show don't tell. Have faith in your characters to deliver the story. You, as the author, should take a back seat.

- Characters should use their senses and so heighten the emotion of any scene.

- Does your story make sense? Have you provided enough information so that the reader understands what's going on? Have you tied up loose threads of the story before the end?

- Is your story leading to a page-turning climax? Have you written a satisfying ending?

- Check for spelling, punctuation and grammar errors.

Exercise 1
Select what you feel is your best piece of writing so far. Edit it closely using the points outlined above.

Exercise 1
Apply the same editing and polishing process to other pieces of work you have written and intend continuing with.

Chapter Fifteen: Inspiration

Step 1: The creative mood

We might have the know-how to write, but we are not always in the mood to write. However, if you sit waiting for inspiration to strike you could be waiting forever. So, when you sit down to write, do just that – write. The creative mood, if it is there at all can be snatched away at the drop of a hat or the slightest interruption. Try not to be a slave to your creative moods. Learn to treat writing as a job. A bricklayer is hardly going to stop laying bricks just because the mood has gone; and a teacher will hopefully not clam up in class because they are no longer in the mood for teaching. Never mind if you are not in a creative mood, just knuckle down and write.

Perseverance

When you are your own boss, it's totally down to you to keep on writing. No one else is going to tell you to get on with your next novel or article or short story. Family and friends will be glad that you're spending time with them, rather than being stuck in your own private world transferring your thoughts onto paper or the screen.

Unless writers can motivate themselves, no one will be doing it for them. And that's possibly why so many talented writers don't go on to be prolific writers with a range of successful pieces of writing to their name.

It takes perseverance, commitment and determination to plough on through all the distractions that life puts in our path. That's not to say writers can't have a family life, a social life and lots of free time – of course we can. If we didn't when would our muse have chance to re-charge and come up with fresh ideas? Not to mentioned gaining inspiration from new places we visit, new information we gather and conversations we have with others.

It's finding that balance, finding time for everything important in our lives. And maybe for those who are pushed to the limits in finding time for writing, then it might be a case of cutting down on the parts of our life which aren't so important, things we do out of habit, or because they are an easy way to pass an hour or two rather than taxing the brain with creative thoughts, or getting back to a writing project.

Prioritising is important. Many would-be novelists put their writing activities to the bottom of the list. They'll get on with their book once they've done the housework, or after they've raked the leaves up from the lawn or gone shopping, or a million and one other distractions. Unless the writer moves their writing further up their list of priorities, the book will never get finished and the next one will never get started.

It's worth remembering that our priorities change day by day. On some days writing time does come last on the list, but on other days you may find it can happily sit top of the list even if only for a few hours.

Getting into the habit of thinking about what you're

writing while you're physically doing other things is a good practice. Plan the next sentence in your story as you're driving to work or doing the shopping. Then, couldn't you quickly scribble it down in that notebook you always carry, once you get to work, or when you've put the shopping back in the car before you drive off? That leaves your mind clear to think up the next sentence and the next as you progress through your day.

This is how books, stories, articles and poems are written. You really don't need a month at a solitary retreat in the back of beyond to be a writer – just a dogged perseverance to keep writing.

The Writing Bug

If you have caught the 'writing bug' then you are probably eager to start writing a novel. It is what most writers seem to aspire to. But remember – don't run before you can walk.

Writing a novel is a massive task, so be sure you are confident and skilled in all the many aspects of writing fiction before setting out on something huge. You need to understand about viewpoint, tense, conflict, characterisation, dialogue, flashbacks etc. And if there is anything you still aren't sure of then study until you have totally grasped it. Then you will be able to concentrate on the important thing – the story.

Writing a novel is time consuming, so be sure that the story you have in mind is one that you are passionate about and feel absolutely dedicated to putting in the time and effort that will be needed to complete it.

Be aware that you will have to do a lot of planning beforehand; a lot of 'note writing' so that you can visualise the setting and understand the background and reasoning of your characters – all of them. You will probably have to do some research – fictional characters have jobs, hobbies, ailments, skills etc., be sure you don't make mistakes when you write about these because your mistakes will be quickly picked up by others in the know.

It is easy to get 'bogged down' with everything when writing a novel, so try and plan a skeleton outline of your story, (even though it may change). This way at least you should not write yourself into a corner.

Step 2: Know the path you are taking

Unless you are free writing, it helps to know what you are writing. It does not *have* to fit into a specific genre, but it will help you to know whether you are writing a short story, flash fiction, a novella or a novel. And from this point whether it's a romance, a crime story, a thriller, a teenage book, a sci-fi story, a horror story, a historical novel or whatever. Try and have your goal in mind as you write.

Take a romantic novel for example: There are different levels of romance ranging from the sweet and sentimental to the erotic; from contemporary to historic, and sub genres within these categories too. There will be a big difference in the readership if you are planning say, a steamy Regency romance or a medical romance. Editors and readers want and expect a different style of writing and content. Reading the sort of books that you want to write will help you target your writing towards the right audience and ultimately improve your chances of publication.

In a nutshell

- Don't wait for inspiration to strike before sitting down to write. You could be waiting forever.

- Prioritise your time so that writing isn't bottom of the list.

- Plan what to write while doing everyday chores, so when you get time to write, you'll be writing – not sitting pondering.

- Don't run before you can walk. Get the basic knowledge and abilities under your belt before tackling something you will struggle with.

- Know what you are writing. Study the different genres out there and have a clear idea what it is you are writing.

- Spend time planning. If you can envisage the scenes throughout your story, and recognize them as milestones in the journey, you will have targets to aim for.

Exercise 1

Take a look at your current work in progress and ask yourself what genre you're aiming towards. Do the same with any other pieces of writing that you've finished – particularly if you've tried to get them published without success.

Exercise 2

If you are struggling to find time to write, analyse your week, and seek out the occasional half hour where you could write instead of your normal pastime.

Chapter Sixteen:
Writer's Block

Step 1: Causes and handling writer's block

I'm sure that all writers, experienced and novice, will get writer's block at some point in their career. In my experience it's different every time. It doesn't just hit you as you're staring at a blank page. Sometimes, you can't even bring yourself to sit down at your computer. Sometimes it can reach a point where you can't even think about the story you're trying to write.

At other times writer's block might hit home when you're getting on well with a story. Suddenly, you don't know where you're going with it. Or maybe you lose confidence in what you've already created and start to doubt yourself as a writer. Writer's block is a real nuisance, and because it strikes you in so many different ways, there's no one simple answer to overcoming it. But let's try.

Let's say you've had a flash of inspiration and you're keen to get writing. Only you can't make up your mind what it's going to be. A factual article, a poem, a short story, a piece of flash fiction, a play, a full-length novel? If you're really confused over what genre your idea falls into, here's some suggestions.

- Mull it over in your head. Go for a long walk and deliberately let your mind concentrate on this idea, see where your thoughts are naturally leading you.

- Working on paper or screen make a 'spider chart' or similar. That is, the initial idea at the centre and a lot of legs or branches coming off, each with a possible thought of where that idea might go.

- Sometimes an idea might seem too huge in your mind and it feels like a complete jumble. With clear planning it helps clarify it so you can hone it down to something manageable.

- Be honest with yourself. If you've got a great idea for a story and you really do want to write an 80,000-word novel – has it got enough *body* and possibilities to reach that length of words? Or really would this make a great novella or short story – or even flash fiction?

- Importantly, don't lose that inspiration. If you want to start writing, then do so. Don't let the practicalities stop you. They can be sorted should you get stuck later.

Let's say writer's block has struck when you are mid-way through a piece of work. To begin with you were filled with enthusiasm. You've sat down and written thousands of words. Ideas of where the story was going were bubbling over. Maybe there were times when you just couldn't get the words down quickly enough. Then inspiration fades, ideas dry up and you're left with a half-finished story. Somehow, you can't find the drive to do anything else about it. So, now what to do?

- If your initial inspiration came from a place you visited, could you re-visit?

- If you can't re-visit, then look up pictures and information about the place.

- If it was a book, a film or a documentary or news story that sparked your idea, re-read or watch again.

- Did you keep a memento in your ideas box, notepad or file from when you got that initial spark? Go and look at it again.

- Read your work again up to the point where you are stuck. Ask yourself why you are stuck:

  - You've written yourself into a dead end.
  - It's a tricky bit of the story which is hard to handle.
  - You've got no idea what happens next.
  - It's become boring.
  - Your characters aren't coming across as intended.
  - You're doubting yourself as a writer.

So, what to do?

You've written yourself into a dead end

Go back and change a character's decision on the action that led to this dead end. It might mean cutting a lot of work out. So, cut out and save in another file – don't delete. You'll probably need it later. But for now, change the course of action and move on. Maybe it's also time to do some bullet point plotting. Try working backwards from how you roughly see the ending, then work logically forwards, until you get close to where you are now.

It's a tricky patch that's hard to handle

Maybe you're stuck at this tricky point because you don't know enough about the subject or character or place. Time then for a break from the book to do some additional research, or some free writing on the character's backstory. If it's too tricky it's fine to jump this section; it's fine to leave a chapter unfinished for now. Move forward and come back to this bit later.

You've got no idea what happens next

Bring in something unexpected, a letter, a phone call, a visitor, another character, an accident, a windfall. Anything to get the story moving again. You can always remove it in the final edit if it really wasn't necessary. Oddly, though, you may find it was important to the story.

It's become boring

If you're finding it boring, the reader will too. So clearly not enough is happening in your character's life. So, again, maybe it's time to bring in another character that will upset the apple cart. Or something unexpected happens. Or you need to go back and alter the course of events. If it's a scene where nothing much is happening, use a transition to jump forward a day or two, or a week or so, to when the action picks up again.

Example: *By the time Aunt Maud arrived the following Sunday, Amy was ready for her...*

Or *The war raged on, Ellie read the newspapers with dread every day as spring turned to summer and autumn turned to winter. The snow was knee deep when the knock came to the door....*

Your characters aren't coming across as intended

If you're not happy with your characters, spend time (in another notebook or file) getting to know them better. Improve on their backstory. Give them problems and hang-ups – with good reason; give them one dark secret; give them a skill or a hobby or a habit; be sure they are driven to achieve something in your story. Be sure they are faced with enough conflict, inner emotional or actual physical. Write throwaway scenes; interview your character. Get to really know them, and make sure they are strongly motivated in your story.

You're doubting yourself as a writer

Join the club! Writers all doubt themselves at some time or other, even the most famous. Take time out to read other writer's blogs to hear about their difficulties. Or just glance to the end of a book and read the author's thanks and praise to the people who have helped and guided them along the way. Try and ignore self-doubt and plough on.

In a nutshell

We all suffer from writer's block at some time or other. If you find yourself in that situation, have a few 'tricks' up your sleeve to give yourself a kick-start.

- Reading an extract from a 'teach yourself' creative writing book often helps, so keep this one close at hand.

- Google some quotes from famous writers about 'writing'.

- Take a break away from your work, do something totally different, such as walking and mull ideas over as you go.

- Try writing some 'throw away' poetry.

- Try some 'free-style' writing. Simply pick random words from the dictionary and write about them without thinking.

- Interview your character, ask them the most random questions and then free write.

- Create a bullet point list of where your story might go. Do more planning.

- Have more than one writing project on the go. Then if one thing isn't working for you, you can switch to something else.

- Don't be too hard on yourself. You are after all trying to conjure something up from nothing, which is amazing if you think about it.

Exercise 1

Hopefully, you'll never suffer from writer's block. But just in case, take time out to find some writer's blogs that you enjoy reading. Jot them down for future reference.

Chapter Seventeen:
Writing for children

Step 1: Know your readership

Many people want to write for children. But if you think that's the easy option towards getting published, think again. Writing for children is equally as hard – if not harder than writing for adults. The children's genre is a very discerning market and competition is high. Even so, the satisfaction in having a children's book published is so worthwhile knowing that you could be setting a young person on the road to a life of loving books and reading.

The very first book I ever had published – not counting some little books on British customs for a Polish publisher, was *Cry Danger* published by Scholastic Children's Books. Prior to being accepted, I had written six other books over as many years – some for adults, which had all been rejected by different publishers. I was elated when I got a phone call to say *Cry Danger* had been accepted. I went on to write another six books for Scholastic before working for other children's publishers.

Incidentally, I'm often asked what happened to the six rejected books. Well, I've re-visited them over the years. Re-writes have resulted in three getting published. The other three are still waiting to be re-written.

The first thing you need to be aware of when considering writing for children is that you can't simply write freely without first thinking about your target readership. The age range when writing for children is huge: babies, toddlers, pre-school, early years, key stages through primary school then senior school, young adults, new adults – until finally you reach books for grown-ups.

If that's not enough, there are cross overs, where your story might be suitable for more than one age group. There are also books for reluctant readers, where the reader might have reached a certain age in years, but their ability to read is at a much lower level. It's surprising what a difference a year can make when writing for children.

It's also worth remembering that publishers, book sellers and librarians need to categorise a book, so they know where to place it on their shelves or in which category online when advertising. Additionally, teachers like to know a book is going to be suitable for their class of pupils. And parents will nearly always be guided by what they see on the market that matches the ages of their children.

Writing your children's story is paved with problems. But when you're the writer and you have a brilliant idea for a children's book, thinking about where it would sit on the bookshelves is probably the last thing on your mind. But if you fail to consider this, then you're likely to fail full stop.

You also need to ensure the story content is right for the

age range. An eight-year-old doesn't want a babyish storyline nor does a three-year-old want to be traumatised by a horror story. The sentence structure and vocabulary also need to be right for the age range. Plus, will the child understand the words you're using? They might able to read the word perfectly well, but do they understand the meaning of it?

I also think writers have a responsibility towards the reader with regard to morals, lessons learnt and so on. And while you want your thrilling book to excite the reader and keep them reading, you don't want to give them nightmares by writing inappropriate scenes or indicating that it pays to be nasty or unkind, and that it's okay to be bad.

Regardless of age, children love stories where they can identify with the characters, even if they are in a different form such as an animal, a fairy, a giant or whatever. The main adventure should be about someone or something with whom they can empathise. Additionally, little ones need the reassurance of their parents being close by. Take note, close by – but not taking over. The young character is the main thing.

Some novice children's writers can't let go of the adult aspect and will write a story where the protagonist is the parent. You have to relinquish the parent being in charge, or the younger characters would never have any adventures or get into mischief. Young readers aren't interested in the parent or the adult's life and activities – keep the parents in the background and let the action revolve around the young protagonist.

As mentioned earlier, there are different categories of books for children. Here's a brief rundown:

Books for babies

These are usually made from thick board or a waterproof, chewable plastic. They might have lift up flaps or be textured and quirky. The illustrations will be bright, simplistic and clear, while the text – if any, will be simple and basic. Topics can be on any number of things: animals, colours, numbers, toys, ABC, food. A written description of what you envisage as the illustration on each page would also be necessary. You would be looking at 8 pages maximum.

Books for babies to age 3

It's never too early to get children interested in books, and books for toddlers need to be bright, bold, colourful and interesting. It's important to realise that you don't need to supply the illustrations. If a publisher likes your story idea and the way you've written it, they will arrange an illustrator.

The themes and subject matter for picture books is immense. Life is just opening up for the child, so topics can range from the everyday things they already know about, such as brushing their teeth and eating peas to a trip to the doctors. Stories can be fantasy, funny, rhyming, have sound effects and moving flaps and tabs.

Despite the young age of the child, the text, while short, can be quite sophisticated as it's being read by an adult.

So, make it fun to read aloud, allow the parent to be expressive and interactive while they read to their child – sounds, singing, nursery rhymes, movement, actions – the books are full of fun. Repetition in picture books is a good thing. The child can join in and start recognising words and phrases.

When submitting a picture book manuscript to a publisher, you would need to set your manuscript out in a picture book format that includes the description of what's going on page-by-page, and the story text, i.e. narrative and dialogue. Usually the page numbers are divisible by 8. But the first few pages are taken up by the publisher, so in essence, your first page would be page 4 or 5.

Age 3 - 5

Still with picture books but now the stories can be more adventurous. The characters can get up to all sorts of exciting things, nothing is beyond them. Nothing is out of reach. A teddy bear who flies to the moon on a toy plane; a boy who can turn pebbles into real dinosaurs; a tiger who comes to tea. The only restriction is your own imagination.

Books can be rhyming or interactive, they can have flaps or bits that move, open out or pop up. At this age, the child may be recognising words, and starting to read themselves. So, simple, basic words and short sentences are required but a captivating story that will encourage them to read more. Themes may be familiar or fantasy, but I would suggest never too scary at this age. And that 'safety blanket' of parents not being too far away is not a bad thing.

Age 5 - 7

The young reader will be at school and learning to read all by themselves. Vocabulary is important and while they may be able to read the words you have written be sure they understand the meaning. If you're going to use a word they may not recognise, phrase it in a way they could take an educated guess at. It's a good thing to expand the young reader's vocabulary, but you don't want the text to be so tricky that it stops the flow of the story and discourages them from reading. As for the story itself, children of this age are interested in everything from magic and dragons to ponies and space ships. However, avoid making it complicated. The child will be having enough trouble learning how to read without trying to work out a complicated plot at the same time. Word length around 2,500.

Age 7 - 9

Books for this age group will have fewer illustrations, perhaps just the occasional line drawing or often none at all. Alternatively, they might be full of line drawings, text and speech bubbles. It might be weird words and fantasy. It might be facts and figures, equations and experiments. Or a straight-forward story. I love writing for this age. There is no limit to what you might write about. The vocabulary you use covers most of the words we use in everyday life, and generally, the child will understand the phrasing that you come up with. Stories now can be longer, anything from 12,000 to 40,000+. They can have more intricate plots, fascinating characters, be more intriguing and more suspenseful. Children at his age want stories that hold their attention, so lots of action, adventure and emotion.

Age 9 – 11

While children all learn at different rates, usually by this age they are generally competent readers, some will be voracious readers. Stories can be on more serious themes, they can be based around real life, around real issues that may concern them or they have heard of. They can be set at any period of history, fact or fiction or a mix of both.

I love writing for this age too because it's fine to write books that send shivers down the spine, although I suggest you hold back on any blood and mindless violence. That won't win you any favours with the editors, parents or teachers. But readers of this age love to be scared and love to laugh. They also love sad and emotional stories. Personally, I'd still go for the happy ending for this age group and the moral outcome of good over bad. Word count: 50,000 or more.

Stories for teens or young adult (YA)

While the young reader by now will be able to read and comprehend to an adult level it needs to be remembered that they are not adults and this should be reflected in the writing of the stories, the theme, the plot and the choice of words. At this age they are inquisitive about everything to do with growing up, so story content could include everyday issues that concern teenagers: families, friendships, relationships, sex, bullying, love, grief and everything in between. The way these subjects are handled however, needs to be done responsibly. They do also like fantasy, romance, horror, adventure, so, plenty of scope here. Word count, 50 – 60,000 or more.

High-Low stories

These stories or books are aimed at older children who have a much lower reading age. Imagine a child of 15 with a reading ability of a five-year-old. You need a story to engage an active, mature teenager, which he or she won't be embarrassed at being seen reading, written in a simple and straightforward way with vocabulary and sentence structure they can cope with. The word length might range from a few hundred to a few thousand words, and the books will often be illustrated.

I've currently written 15 reluctant reader books for educational publisher Badger Learning, with two titles winning awards. (*Keeper* and *A Little Secret*). The story is the thing. Come up with a great story a young person of that age will love – regardless of their reading ability. Keep the plot straightforward, avoid flashbacks and complicated threads; and then re-write it using simpler words and phrases.

Step 2: Illustrations for children's books

You won't be expected to supply the illustrations for children's books. Publishers have their own stable of illustrators who they call on to provide the pictures. However, if you are an artist first and foremost, then this should be established with potential publishers when first submitting your ideas or your manuscript. If a publisher or editor is interested they will guide you as to what illustrations are required and how they should be submitted. Therefore, it would be best to just do sample illustrations for your book, rather than the entire artwork for the story, as editors tend to have their own ideas.

If you are self-publishing a picture book, the illustrations would eventually need to be saved as jpgs, or in a format that your print company requires. On-line self-publishing platforms such as KDP Amazon have full instructions as to how to go about this. And as technology is marching on, then checking the way of doing this needs to be looked at once you are ready to go ahead with your project.

Step 3: Finding inspiration for your children's book

Like any genre, you need a spark of inspiration to begin with. Something that tells you it's a great idea for a book. Inspiration for children's books is all around us: real life, history, the world, the planets and stars, nature, science, space. Now, once you have your spark, ask yourself:

- Do you envisage only a few words to go with colourful pictures?

- Is your idea quirky, short or rhyming?

- Do you want the child to read it themselves or be read to?

- Do you have a plot in mind? How complicated is that plot?

- What is the conflict in the story?

- How old is the main character in your story?

- Does the adventure suit the readership you have in mind? Young readers will prefer to look up to the main character, so someone of around the same age or a little older – not younger would be required.

- Can you estimate the number of words in your story: under 100, 500, 1,000, 7,000, 12,000, 24,000, 40,000, or more?

When you know who your intended reader is, then it's time to begin plotting, planning and writing, precisely as you would if writing for an adult. There are no shortcuts on creating characters, writing dialogue, devising a great plot, describing a location, bringing in the tension and emotion, editing and re-writing just because it's for young readers.

Whether you are writing for a one-year-old or a 19-year-old, the quality of your writing must be the very best you can do. Don't think you can forget the craftsmanship of good writing just because it's for a toddler. All the rules and laws of writing fiction still apply:

- A beginning, a middle and an end (ideally).

- Conflict – conflict that will suit the readership.

- Narrative that paints a picture.

- Make every word count.

- Good dialogue which is believable for that character.

- Start where something different is happening.

- Reach the point in your story where it looks like the character isn't going to overcome their problems.

- Let there be a resolution to the conflict – in other words, let the character achieve their goals – or not. It doesn't have to be a happy ending for older children but be sure it's a satisfactory ending in some way. However, for young readers, I'd suggest you go for a happy ending.

- Avoid 'writing down' to the child. Credit them with intelligence for their years.

Keep that young reader in mind as you're writing. Or better still allow yourself to become that reader and see the world through their eyes.

In a nutshell

- Don't be mistaken in thinking writing for children is easier than writing for adults. If anything, it's harder. It's not just the reader you're aiming to please, but parents, teachers and librarians too.

- Read and become familiar with children's books for all ages. Know and understand what they are reading.

- Know who you are writing for. Know the age group and ability. Write to suit. Select the content and theme that will interest readers of that age. Use vocabulary suitable for the age range

- Remember an 8-year-old doesn't really want a 6-year-old protagonist. Make your main character around the same age or slightly older than the reader. Avoid mentioning the character's age if possible – why restrict yourself?

- Make it the child's story. Keep parents and other

adults in the background, unless of course, they are vital to the plot.

- As with fiction for any age, ensure you have believable characters; make sure you are 'showing not telling'; make the dialogue sparkle; choose your viewpoint characters carefully and don't 'head hop'; don't allow your narrative to slow the story down, keep the story moving at a good pace; make use of cliff hangers at chapter endings.

- Become familiar with different children's publishers. Keep an eye on their websites, watch out for submission requests.

Exercise 1

As an exercise in writing for different age groups, write the following scene twice. Firstly, so that it suits a six-year-old child who is just starting to read by himself, and then to suit a 12-year-old reader. Scenario: *Jack is walking through thick mud and his boots become stuck.*

Exercise 2

Try writing this scene for a toddler where an adult is reading to the child; then write the scene with a 15-year-old reader in mind. Scenario: *Sally is in the park contemplating going on the swings and slides.*

Treat yourself to a copy of Karen King's book: *Get Writing Children's Fiction.*

Chapter Eighteen: Writing short stories

Step 1: The short story

The short story is a most versatile genre of writing to tackle. There are no restraints on the subject, the length or the style. Of course, if you have a target market in mind, or a competition you're trying for, there will be rules and guidelines for you to comply with. But if you are writing a short story for your own enjoyment, then you're as free as a bird.

The beauty of a short story is that it can usually be read in one sitting. A good short story often seems so easy, so simple. When you read a short story and think how simple it was, that's a good thing. No one wants to be trying to work out what the author is trying to say, nor do they want to be bamboozled by obscure words and phrases. They want the story. And because it reads easily, you can bet your life that it wasn't thrown down on the page easily. The writer will most certainly have grafted for long hours, days, weeks or even months.

The length of a short story varies from around 700 words to 7-8,000 words. Shorter than 700 and it is usually classed as flash fiction. A story of between 2,100 to 2,400 words would fit into a 15-minute radio short story slot. In general, magazine stories range from around 1,000 – 3,000 words. But if you have a publication in mind, check the word length they prefer and stick to it.

Many journals offer fiction guidelines.

If you want to write short stories, then read as many as you can. For a particular market, study published stories to get a feel for the style and content. Analyse those stories. Look to see the usual number of characters involved in a typical story and whether they are usually written from one viewpoint or more. Are they *twist in the tale?* Look at the age range of characters and their lifestyles. Usually when a magazine has been printing a certain type of short story for years and it is still popular, they aren't looking for change. So, there's little point in trying to break the mould with a story that is totally alien to their usual style.

Short story competitions might provide a wider scope for your work, so keep your eyes peeled for competitions. There are always lots about and prize money can be well worth winning, not to mention the esteem of being placed in a competition – great for your morale. Read competition rules carefully and abide by them.

There is an art in writing the short story. You have to get such a lot in within a relatively short number of words. You have to open with a 'punch', grab the reader at once, set the scene, establish the conflict, show the personality of the character and get the reader to immediately care that they have a problem. Phew!

Give your story structure: a beginning, a middle and an end. It's a short story, it should start and it should finish, and it should leave the reader feeling all the better for reading it. Hopefully you will have given the reader something to think about and maybe even made a lasting impression on them.

You might want to write a twist in the tail story, but unless you have a great beginning – something that will hook the reader and keep them reading, they will never reach that surprise ending.

Begin your story where something is happening. Cut away the preamble and get straight to the heart of the matter. Keep it interesting. Remember to *show* not *tell* in your story. Be economical with description. It's a short story, and unless you're writing about something that isn't known to man, you don't have to describe everyday normal things and places. Leave something to the reader's imagination and concentrate on the characters and the action of your story. Make sure your protagonist is facing some sort of problem or dilemma. Every story must have conflict – emotional, physical or both. Things happen in short stories.

Usually short stories are written from a single viewpoint – the story is told through the eyes and feelings of your protagonist. You need a strong storyline or plot, there is no time to meander aimlessly, the reader wants to know what is happening here and now.

Nevertheless, you must write the story in a way that it is a pleasure to read. Your words must paint a picture, reflect the mood. It should flow. It should almost appear easy – effortless, when in fact you will have worked very hard to achieve that ease of reading.

Provide a good ending. If there's a twist, let it be

believable. If you can leave the reader with something that is thought-provoking, all the better.

Remember to re-write. Cut out all superfluous words. Re-phrase to make the story more concise. Make every word of dialogue have earned its right to be there. Read your story aloud. Listen to the flow of your sentences. If they don't flow, tweak them so they do.

Step 2: What makes a short story?

An original idea

A tall order to start with and you would be forgiven for thinking that there are no original ideas left under the sun. Except *you* are an original, and your writing is unique to you, so put your individual stamp on an idea and create something fresh and new. Be sure however that the idea excites you. Otherwise it's not going to excite anyone else either.

Believable characters

The short story revolves around its characters, so let your protagonist's problem be established early on. Reveal the conflict they are facing by writing through their viewpoint. Use dialogue to reveal personality and moods as well as to carry the story forward. Make sure that every word of that dialogue is there for a purpose.

A realistic setting

When writing to the restrictions of a word count, the luxury of rambling descriptions and narrative is not an option. Find ways of revealing the background by your succinct writing. Nevertheless, you must still set the scene convincingly to engage your readers.

An intriguing beginning

Begin with the action in full flow. Set the scene, introduce the character and establish the conflict. Aim to grab the reader immediately and keep the story moving forward by ensuring there are no wasted words or unnecessary scenes or dialogue.

Conflict

Whether the conflict your protagonist is facing is physical or emotional, or both, let it be clear what they are up against. Get the reader on side with your main character, so they are rooting from the very start for the protagonist to achieve their goal.

Suspense

I am not suggesting continual breath-taking drama and heart-racing action, the suspense can be the anxiety or turmoil in the protagonist's mind. So, try to keep the reader in suspense by them not knowing what your character is going to do to overcome their difficulties. Keep that momentum going.

Structure

The beginning, where you introduce your characters – not too many; set the scene and indicate the conflict. The middle, where the action develops with ever increasing interest. And the end where we see the problem resolved one way or the other. Keep the time span short and avoid extending your story to an anti-climax with the tying up of loose ends. Ensure loose ends are all resolved before the climax.

A satisfying ending

Happy endings are not compulsory – although your market research may show otherwise. In any case, make sure your ending leaves the reader satisfied and not left feeling puzzled or cheated. An unexpected but totally believable ending is always good.

In a nutshell

- If you have a target market in mind, check out the guidelines. Likewise, if entering a short story competition, read the rules and stick to them.

- The idea of a short story is that it can be read in one sitting. So, you only have a limited time to create a lasting impression on the reader's mind.

- Think about the effect you want to achieve and keep that in mind with every word you write.

- Start where something different is happening.

214

Grab the reader from the first paragraph. Cut away the preamble and get straight to the heart of the matter.

- Create believable characters.

- Provide events the readers can't easily foretell.

- Make sure the story flows nicely.

- Let your words, descriptions and phrasing paint a picture.

- Make sure your ending is unexpected rather that predictable.

- Your work should be well presented, neat, without spelling and punctuation mistakes.

- You might be writing a twist in the tail story but don't rely on your brilliant ending to sell your story. The editor might not get that far.

- Be economical with description. It's a short story, so don't waste words on the mundane; focus on aspects that really matter.

- Re-write and re-phrase. Cut out all superfluous words. Make every word fight for its right to be there.

- Read your story aloud. Listen to the rhythm and flow of your sentences. If they don't flow, tweak until they do.

Exercise 1
Research the marketplace for possible outlets for your short stories, including online magazines. Also, check out current short story competitions. Note the closing dates and read the rules carefully.

Exercise 2
Sketch out a skeleton plot or outline for a short story for a publication/competition which appeals to you. Develop this into a short story and submit it.

Chapter Nineteen:
Writing about yourself

Step 1: Biographies, autobiographies and family history

Lots of people think about writing their own life story, many have successfully done so. A great many autobiographies become best sellers – and they are not all written by celebrities. Many are written by ordinary people who have lived remarkable lives. If you plan on writing your life story, or a biography of someone you know, then read as many as you can to see how they are crafted. Look at the chronologic layout of the books. See what makes them interesting and readable.

Writing your autobiography, or someone else's biography takes careful planning. It would be so easy to get bogged down with all the research necessary – a lifetime's activities, achievements and conversations. Likewise, if you're planning on writing a book about your family history – such a project could take years. The research and how to go about it is way beyond the scope of this writing guide. But be aware that you would need to do copious amounts of research, fact finding, and the gathering of documents and photographs. It's only when you have all this information together, and you're ready to start writing your book, that you can begin to plan and plot, and mould all that information into something readable.

Step 2: Visualise your book

Ask yourself how you visualise your completed family history, biography or autobiography. Will it be a simple photocopied booklet to give to family members, or a full scale professionally published, illustrated book? If the latter is your choice, unless you have an amazing family saga to tell, and the ability to write it in a way that publishers will be fighting over it, you will probably struggle to find a publisher. But of course, if the book is really mainly for yourself and family, you can self-publish.

Pick out the highlights, the low spots, the joyous and the sorrowful times, the important landmark events that were life changing. Let your mind slip back to occasions that you can remember vividly so you can write them with colour and emotion and really paint a picture of that moment in time for others to see.

While you may intend writing it in chronological order, your mind may have other ideas. Incidents and conversations will probably be popping up in your head at the least convenient time, so be sure to have notebooks at the ready to jot down your thoughts. If you are writing about one period in time and your thoughts suddenly jump forward a decade or two, then write it as it occurs to you. Those thoughts may never come back as vividly. Note the change of time and place, log it down and find your own way of keeping track. Coloured pens may help or different fonts or highlighted coloured paragraphs.

This is certainly one style of book that is not straight forward to write. However, like any book, it must be written in a way that engages the reader and interests them enough to keep reading. Vary the emotions, a happy scene might follow a sad scene or vice versa. It is doubtful you will recall actual conversations, but dialogue will bring your book to life, just as in any fictional book. The reader may lose interest in a book that is purely narrated from start to finish.

Writing your family history is a wonderful legacy for your family, relatives and descendants as well as being a fascinating project to embark upon. It is also a huge task to attempt. The very thought of which may daunt you from even making a start. However, if you take it step by step, you will find the path easier.

Step 3: What format will it take?

Depending on the material you have to work with, decide on the format of your book. If you have lots of photographs, then you might want to plan your story as a gallery of images mingled with text as you write the stories and anecdotes that are associated with the pictures. Maybe the material you have includes diaries and letters, so you might plan to publish these along with your narrative to set the scene.

Scope

Decide upon the scope of your story. You might want to begin with the earliest known ancestor and follow him/her down through a single line of descent to present day. You could devote each chapter to each ancestor or each generation or line of descent. Alternatively, you might want to start with the present day and work back in time. But again, plot your chapters accordingly and have a method of working and keeping track so that it doesn't become too confusing.

You'll need to list all the incident that you can remember. Include events from childhood and parents. You'll need to write about your school days, your teenage years, your working life and your love life. Health issues may come into it, along with births and deaths, marriages and divorces.

Think beyond the family to characters who have been influential in some way – teachers, work colleagues, friends. Of course, not every person or incident will make the final edit. But in the planning stages, it's best not to forget anyone.

Step 4: Research

You want readers to enjoy your family history so try not to make it just a dull list of dates and names. Your readers need to experience these people's lives. So, find out what their daily lives must have been like through research. Even if you cannot find exact details of individual ancestors, you will be able to find out what was going on at the time in history, maybe even weather conditions if you can find freak storms or hottest summers recorded. You should be able to find out what living conditions were like, cost of foods, what was available and what was not – all kinds of things to bring your story to life.

Look at the political scene at the time; look at timelines for major events such as wars, epidemics and disasters which may have had an influence at the time. Look at fashions, food, modes of transport, entertainment of the day. Research your ancestors' occupations so you can describe what their day to day life was like. Interview living relatives to get their personal memories and so add colour to your story.

Step 5: Plot and theme

You might choose to give your story a plot and theme. Maybe it will be a rags to riches story or a tale of survival against the odds. You might discover that your family crosses from one country to another in search of a better life. Or maybe your story is based around a family trade. Just like fictional stories, family history stories need a plot and theme too.

Step 6: Consider the title

You may find choosing the title of your book to be easy. It might have been with you throughout the months (or years) that you've been researching and gathering facts. Or you might struggle to find the right title. Ideally keep it in line with the tone and theme of your book. Keep it short and memorable. If it's an autobiography you could simply have your name followed by – *My Story*. You could also browse similar books and look at their titles for inspiration. Or perhaps two or three poignant words from your book would make a fitting title.

Step 7: The starting point

This is entirely your decision. Your story does not have to start at the earliest or most distant time in your research and work forwards in time. Nor does it have to start at the present day and work backwards. You could take one line of the family tree and write at length about them before switching to another branch of the family tree. You could choose an interesting fact or anecdote about an ancestor and begin with that if you wanted. The main thing is to start at a point which will grab your reader and interest them.

Step 8: The content

Writing about yourself and people you know can be a tricky business. Be aware that writing anything libellous will get you into trouble. The last thing you want is to be sued. It doesn't even have to be libellous, anything you write about people who are still around to read it, or who have family or descendants who might take exception to what you've written, can lead to problems for you. If you're quoting someone, you'd be wise to get their permission to do so. Think about the consequences before you start dragging skeletons out of the cupboards for the whole world to read about.

You need to get your facts right. When writing about real people and real events you need to double check everything. The memory can play tricks, so don't rely on your memory over things that can be checked up on.

Be aware too, that if you're writing a true story, then it needs to be the truth, and not written in a way that bends the truth or alters history, or changes the course of events or the personality of someone – and that includes yourself.

Step 9: Your writing voice

Finding your writing voice should come naturally to you. If it's your autobiography, then write it from the heart, so that the reader gets to know you. After all, that's what the book is about. As in any fictional story, this book also needs to see the problems, the difficulties and the heartaches. The reader needs to feel the emotion as you write about important scenes and events throughout your life.

The story needs structure too, as it rises in drama or suspense, climbing towards the climax of your story. And the ending should bring some resolution – some understanding of the life that has been led, lessons learned and some acceptance. Maybe a wistful look back, or a bright prospect of the future.

Step 10: Editing your biography

It would be a good idea to let some trusted people read your book before sending it to a publisher or going for the self-publishing route. We are always too close to our writing, and never more so than when writing about ourselves or family members. What you might consider a hilarious anecdote might be totally boring to someone else. Another person may also be aware of aspects you've accidentally – or deliberately left out. To that reader this may feel like a gaping hole in the plot which needs addressing. If more than one person picks on something that needs attention, then it's worth taking a closer look at what you've written – or not written.

If you're planning on self-publishing, then getting a copy editor to work on your manuscript is a necessity so that you can go forward and publish your book with confidence.

In a nutshell

- Be prepared for copious amounts of research.

- Envisage the style of book you want.

- Plan the order in which you'll be writing it.

- Start with an incident that will hook and intrigue the reader.

- Write from the heart and be true to yourself.

224

- Make sure your facts are correct.

- Don't shy away from emotional moments.

- Be sure you've covered the important eras.

- Check for anything libellous.

- Make sure your book is edited to a professional standard.

Exercise 1
Even if you have no plans to write and publish your autobiography, as an exercise write a list of the highlights you would cover if you were writing such a book.

Exercise 2
Think of a happy or a humorous time in your life, and write this up, bringing as much colour and emotion as you can.

Chapter Twenty: Writing a Novel

Step 1: Taking the plunge

Writing a novel is what many writers aspire to. It's the dream. And if you've mastered all the techniques of writing so far, there's no reason for you not to tackle writing your first novel.

So, where to start? Well, as with anything, you need an idea – and it needs to be an idea that excites you and interests you, because you're going to be spending a lot of time thinking about it and working on it. And if you're not excited by the prospect, then it's not going to work.

So, armed with your brilliant idea for a book, it's time to get down to some planning. Firstly, know what sort of book it is you are writing. As mentioned previously, it's important to know what genre you're writing for. Is it a detective story, a western, a romance, a child's book, a YA book or any of the other genres? Know what it is you are writing.

Jumping ahead for a moment to the next chapter, you'll see it's on writing the synopsis, which is what you'll be asked for when you get to the stage of sending your manuscript off to possible publishers and agents. However, at this stage it might help you when you're planning your story, for you to write yourself a very loose synopsis. This synopsis is purely for you. Not for a publisher or anyone else to see. This is your outline for your story. Make it as brief or as detailed as you like. This will really help you to get to know your story. And it will help you to navigate your way through your story when you get down to writing it in earnest.

You can refer to this synopsis or outline continually as you begin writing your book. For one thing it may help keep you on track. You can also add notes and possible scenes to it whenever they occur to you. If you have a written outline of your novel, it leaves your mind free to work on the detail without trying to hold the entire story in your head.

Step 2: Planning and developing your novel

If you've been enthused enough to already have started, then don't let me stop you. Strike while the iron is hot. But at some point, you will need to plot and structure your story. I would advise that you start working on this before you write yourself into a corner, because if you suddenly hit a dead end in your writing, and writer's block sets in, it may stop the flow for a considerable time. So, stay in control and get some building blocks laid out.

You need to have decided what tense and person you're writing in. This might come naturally to you the moment you start writing, or you might need to have some trial runs, to discover what seems the most natural. You also need to decide whose viewpoint you are writing the story through. And if you're having more than one viewpoint character, work out where the viewpoint changes will need to come.

Make time to develop your characters, in particular your protagonist. Work on their background because this will influence how they are now. And if you're created a history for this character, he or she will come across as a fully fleshed out character, not a cardboard cut-out. Remember to give them abilities and flaws. Don't make them too perfect, but also remember that you want the reader to identify and empathise with them. Unless you get the reader to care about your protagonist, they won't care about your book.

Your character needs to be aiming to achieve something and there needs to be obstacles getting in their way. Whatever conflict it is, make it important. Make the goal it life changing in some way. If it's trivial, then it won't grab the reader. Make it really matter. Remember too, that you need different layers of conflict – emotional as well as actual physical difficulties, and keep the problems coming. Let it be one thing after another for your protagonist to deal with. And let the problems keep mounting up, heading towards the dramatic climax of the story towards the end of the book when it appears that your protagonist is going to fail.

Make the journey through the story a lively one. If there are passages that seem dull to you, they will also be dull to the reader. Make every paragraph a joy to read with your style and use of phrasing and vocabulary.

Knowing where to start can be a puzzle, so start where something new is happening in your protagonist's life, some change, or something major they need to get to grips with. Remember that you want to hook the reader at the start and make them want to read on. Remember too, that you don't have to reveal everything at the start. Let the reader uncover what you want them to know at your pace, rather than bombarding them with masses of names and information all at once.

The rate you progress is all down to you. You might find that you like to perfect each section before moving on, or alternatively, you might just want to plough on with the story with a view to editing it later. There's no right or wrong way, every writer is an individual. You need to discover what feels right to you.

If you create believable characters and establish them in their own world, their obstacles will be founded within the framework of their home or lifestyle, and it will involve people who are in their world. You won't have to go looking for events, action and conflict in some contrived way. Your plot will be led by the characters.

Your characters need to be passionate about their own beliefs and needs, and this applies to all of your characters, and especially to those who your protagonist comes into contact with mostly. Make this person or persons equally as passionate about their desires – good or bad. If you have them opposite or contradictory to your main character's aims, then you have a good story.

Your conflict doesn't necessarily have to be obviously

right/wrong, good/bad. Two opposing characters can have genuinely positive ambitions or goals, and each one has an important reason for achieving their goal. It doesn't mean that one's right and the other wrong. But whatever goals your characters have, make them worth fighting for – make them life changing. Make it *really* matter if they don't succeed.

Throughout your story, remember to show not tell. Let the reader be as close to the action as possible – and that means being inside the viewpoint character's head, understanding their thoughts and emotions. Let the reader live each scene in the book.

Know in your mind what the climax of your story is to be and be continually heading in that direction, so the pressure is kept on with things getting worse and worse for the protagonist. You'll know where that climax is coming – almost at the end of your story. Don't let the most dramatic thing happen halfway through your story, or the rest will be an anti-climax.

As you're approaching the climax, start tying up those loose ends and sub plot threads. This leaves you free to really concentrate on the climax of the story. The point where your protagonist seems doomed to failure. Take the story to the point where the readers can see no way out for him or her. Then, your protagonist's actions, thoughts, deeds or words are what turns the situation upside down and bring this to a conclusion.

The resolution is what follows – what the protagonist has learned from all this, and how their life will be from this point on. Be brief here, and as mentioned above, don't start tying all the loose ends up now. That should have been done before the climax.

The ending – happy or not? That's up to you. Everybody loves a happy ending but depending upon the sort of novel you're writing, people also like the shock ending, or a dramatic twist, or a heart-breaking ending. Whatever you choose, try and make it memorable and satisfying for the reader.

Step 3: Editing your novel

Writing a novel can take many months, and even years in some cases. But when the moment finally comes when you type the words *The End,* it's certainly a reason for celebration. Writing a novel is a great achievement. But, it's not the end of your work.

Put your manuscript aside for as long as possible before returning to it with fresh eyes. Then, try reading it through with a notebook at hand to jot down areas which need extra work. See if the characters come across as real people. Have you got them behaving in a manner that is logical to them? Is the story believable? Have you got the tension rising – emotional tension as well as the overall action of the story? Are the characters coming across in the ways that you intended? Is it too wordy – could you re-phrase for better effect? Do any parts bore you? Look out for head-hopping, repetition, author telling. Are you loving reading it? If you are, chances are the reader will too.

After all this work, it's time to edit your story. Time to re-work the parts that need re-working. Don't skip this part of the process. It may not be easy, but re-work anything that seems even slightly wrong or out of sync.

If you have some trusted readers whose opinion you value, ask them to read your manuscript and give you some feedback. Take note of their comments, and if you agree, make the necessary changes. But you have to be the one who is happy with the book. Be true to yourself. If an editor suggests changes, that's a different matter. Editors have lots of experience and they wield the power over whether they publish or not. If you have a good working arrangement with your editor, it certainly helps for a harmonious process.

When you are finally finished, it's time to look at the presentation of your manuscript and approaching a publisher. Good luck!

In a nutshell

- Don't run before you can walk. Make sure you understand the basics of writing fiction before embarking on a huge project such as writing a novel. You don't want to be making the same basic mistakes over and over again.

- Your idea must excite you. You'll be working on your book for months, so make sure you can hold onto your enthusiasm for all that time.

- I would advise planning, plotting and structuring your story, to avoid writer's block. Write a synopsis just for you so you can see where your story is going.

- When it comes to writing your book, bring in all your writing techniques and acquired skills. Refer back to this guide as often as you like.

- It's a long haul, so try writing a bit every day. A couple of pages per day will soon mount up.

- Don't shirk on the editing process. This makes all the difference between an average story and a great story.

- Take constructive criticism onboard and look to improve – particularly if the advice is offered by an editor.

Exercise 1

Do some market research into what book publishers are looking for at the moment.

Exercise 2

If you feel ready to start writing a book, then go ahead with the initial planning. Take it all a step at a time – and enjoy the process.

Chapter Twenty-One: Writing the Synopsis

Step 1: The dreaded synopsis

Most publishers will ask for sample chapters and a synopsis and I have yet to meet a writer who enjoys writing the synopsis. For some writers, the dreaded word 'synopsis' strikes fear into their hearts. Yet ask that writer what their story is about, and there will be no stopping them.

Explaining your story is totally different than trying to write it. You can talk at your leisure, re-capping or explaining further if need be. Your explanation can be as long or as short as you like, judging by the other person's interest. You can add your own flair and enthusiasm to the explanation – all things that can't be done in a written, formal synopsis.

That written synopsis for an editor or agent could be what stands between you and success. It's vital that you get it right. A lot is riding on this, so naturally it's scary.

The problem with writing a synopsis is knowing how much to put in and deciding what to leave out. And just how long should a synopsis be anyway?

Basically, a synopsis is an explanation of your story from beginning to end – but in a nutshell. I find it's best to write it in the present tense. The length of a synopsis may vary anything from half a page to 10 pages or more. It depends on what the publisher asks for. If they don't specify the length, aim to write it within two or three pages. Don't allow it to be rambling. Make every word count. It should be as well written as your actual book and flow equally well.

It needs to tell the entire story, from beginning to end including the dramatic high spots and the ending. It needs to say whose story it is (the protagonist) and who the other important characters are. It should portray the intensity and flavour of your book and give an account of the main characters, their goals, conflict they face and what they stand to lose if they fail in their endeavours.

As you write your synopsis don't forget the emotional angle. Don't just write about what your protagonist is doing, but what they are feeling, and how those emotions are changing as the story progresses.

The editor will want to know the dramatic high and low spots, and the dramatic climax to the story and how it ends. Yes, they want to know how it ends. The synopsis is not the blurb where you're teasing the reader. Let the editor know how it ends, and how this affects the protagonist.

Be prepared to write your synopsis over and over. Your first efforts will no doubt be long and complicated. Be aware that if you put in too much detail and complications it could lead to confusion.

Remember to edit and polish your synopsis until it sparkles before sending it off. You could also read it to a trusted friend or family member who doesn't know the story to see if it all makes sense to them. Take note of any feedback.

In your covering letter you should state the approximate length of your book, and who you think the story will appeal to – particularly when writing for children, be specific with the age group you are aiming for. Give a brief account of yourself regarding your writing career (a sentence or two – not your life story).

As with anything, practice makes perfect. So, the more synopses you write, the more confident you'll feel about them.

In a nutshell

- The editor will want to know what genre it is.

- An approximate word length.

- Where and when the story is set.

- Who the major characters are.

- What are the goals of the major characters and what's stopping them from achieving their aims? Also, what's at stake if they don't succeed?

- The editor will want to know the major highs and lows in the story and how it's resolved. Yes, the editor will want to know how your story ends.

- The editor will also want to see how the character has developed emotionally.

- Don't complicate your synopsis. Too much detail leads to confusion.

- It's best to write the synopsis in the present tense.

- Spend time editing and re-working, remove superfluous words.

- Read aloud. Read to a trusted friend who doesn't know the story. Take on board their feedback.

Exercise 1
If you're working on a story – long or short, write a synopsis of it as a practise exercise.

Exercise 2
Choose a published book that you know well and write a synopsis about this as practice.

Chapter Twenty-Two:
Getting your book published

Step 1: Presentation

As mentioned throughout this book, presentation is so important. After putting so much effort into writing your book be sure you don't let yourself down by presenting it to a publisher or editor in anything but a totally professional way.

To reiterate, type or print on A4 paper or in a word document, double spaced unless the publisher's guidelines say otherwise, with good margins all around. Choose an easy to read font such as Times Roman Numeral, font size 12. In the header or footer, number each page, ideally with a word of your name, a word of the title and the page number: E.g. *Writer/Evans/238* I usually do this in a smaller font.

Make sure your work is free from spelling and punctuation mistakes. Most word processing programmes highlight spelling and punctuation errors, so take note of any underlining, and work out what it's telling you. Don't rely on this however, and it shouldn't be used as a replacement for understanding English grammar.

Include a covering page with your manuscript giving the title, number of words, your name, your address and contact details. Also include a brief covering letter or email saying what is enclosed or attached.

Most editors prefer submissions by email, or sometimes through a submission form on their website. Check their preference. If your work is to be sent as hard copy through the post, send it in a sturdy envelope addressed to the correct person. You could include a stamped self-addressed postcard for them to acknowledge receipt of your manuscript. Or include return postage if you want your manuscript back.

Step 2: Approaching publishers and editors

It goes without saying that different publishers publish different types of books. Be sure to do your research before sending your manuscript off. Check out *The Writers' & Artists' Yearbook* and browse bookshops and libraries to see who is publishing what. Look at selected publishers' websites and catalogues to see what they have published in the past and what they are currently publishing.

Publishing houses have various ways of working. Many only agree to look at manuscripts if they are submitted by a literary agent. Some prefer an enquiry letter first, others will look at a few chapters and a synopsis, and some may want to see the whole manuscript. Your research will determine how each one likes to be approached. In every instance, however, be sure to write your preliminary letter or email with the utmost care.

Step 3: Getting a publishing contract

To get your first publishing contract for a book is the most wonderful moment of any writer's life. It's a dream come true. But once the feelings of euphoria have calmed a little then it's time to read the contract carefully – a number of times.

Undoubtedly, the official jargon will be daunting, and if you have a literary agent, or you're a member of The Society of Authors, The Writers' Guild or the National Union of Journalists, you will be able to get guidance from them. If there's anything you're not certain about, or not happy with, then you could get back to the publisher for clarification. You will also find guidance in *The Writers' & Artists' Yearbook*. Although I seem to be mentioning this reference book a lot, it is a really useful source of information for writers.

Only sign your contract when you understand fully what you're agreeing to. Primarily:

- What rights the author is granting to the publisher in terms of territory and the forms of publishing. E.g. hardback, paperback, digital, audio, film etc.

- The author's responsibilities to the publisher such as when the manuscript will be finished and delivered.

- The publisher's responsibilities to the author covering the editing, cover, timeframe for publication, promotion, complimentary copies of the book they will receive.

- Payment to the author including details of the Advance if there is to be one, and Royalties – percentages, plus when and how often royalties will be paid.

- The length of time the author is under contract to that publisher. And what happens if either party wishes to terminate the contract.

When you are happy with the contract, you sign both copies and return to the publisher, who in turn signs them, keeps one and sends the other back to you or your agent.

Don't think that your job is now done, and you can sit back and wait for fame and fortune to come knocking on the door. There is more hard work to be done.

Step 4: The edits

Next comes the edits, which may come as a shock. These professional edits and suggestions from your editor will be on a totally new level to your own editing process. Most likely you will eventually receive an edited copy of your manuscript. And most likely it will be littered with 'track changes' and suggestions from your editor.

If this is your first book, this will come as a shock. And as you go through the changes there could be moments when you think the editor actually hates your book. They don't. Try to look at it like a caring parent wanting the best for their child, painful though it is.

The editing process can go on for quite some time, with different versions passing back and forth between author and editor, until both are finally happy.

After that point, you will eventually get the 'proofs' of your book. These are for you to check meticulously. As once these are approved, the next stage will be your book going to print. This isn't the point to be making radical changes to the story, but it is the point to look for the tiniest little errors – a missing comma, a misspelt word and so on.

Meanwhile, you may also have been approached regarding the cover. Some publishers involve the author in the process, some don't. You will get to see it (usually) before you see the finished book, and hopefully you will love it. If there is a problem with it, then contact your publisher straight away. With my very first book, there was an issue with the cover picture. My character needed red hair, not dark brown. It was crucial to the story. Happily, they agreed, and the cover was changed.

Step 5: Promoting your book

A good publisher will have a marketing/publicity team or person who will be busy raising awareness of your book. However, you as the author will be expected to do as much as you can too.

Make use of social media. Have a presence on as many platforms as you can: Facebook, Twitter, Instagram, Linked in, Goodreads, Amazon's Author Central etc. Create a website, start a blog. Your publisher may organise a blog tour and send copies of your book to reviewers to create a real buzz and excitement about your book well before it is released.

Once your book is out there, you or your publisher can organise book signings at bookshops and libraries. You might choose to arrange talks for various book clubs, writing groups and societies. You could arrange a launch party – and even an online launch party. The publication of your book can be a real whirlwind of activity and excitement. And why not? This is what you've been working towards. Enjoy every moment. And then get on with writing the next book.

Step 6: Beware of vanity publishing

When looking for a publisher, be very careful not to get coerced into going for vanity publishing. This term is applied to a publisher who promises to publish your book for X amount of pounds – which can run into thousands. The publishing house certainly will not be advertising themselves as vanity publishers, they will find other terms to describe their method of work.

So, as stressed previously, read your contract very carefully, take advice. Do your own research into the publisher if it's one you haven't heard of before. Check out the books they say they have published. A quick search on Amazon will reveal the truth. Search online for any negative comments. Check out their social media presence, see what they are posting, and see what people are saying in return.

If you do go down the vanity publishing route and end up paying hundreds or thousands of pounds, and they do deliver the books – it's been known that some vanity publishers don't come up with the goods, then be aware that pricing your vanity published book will have to be quite high if you are ever to recoup your outgoing costs. This in turn will make it difficult for you to sell your book. Plus, you might find it difficult getting it into bookshops.

There's more advice about avoiding vanity publishers in *The Writers' & Artists' Yearbook.* Invest in a copy, it will be money well spent.

Step 7: Author assisted publishing

Some publishers offer 'author assist' publishing, where the author chips in with a certain amount of money towards the costs of publishing. It's entirely up to you whether or not you choose to pay to get your book published but make sure you know exactly what you're getting for your money. But be aware that you can self-publish.

In a nutshell

- Getting your book published is a real possibility.

Consider your options whether to look for a traditional publisher or to self-publish. More on self-publishing in the next chapter.

- Be aware that your manuscript should be free of spelling and grammatical errors; and while a traditional publisher will allocate an editor to work on your book if they accept it, if you self-publish this responsibility falls to you.

- If you get a contract, study it well and take proper advice before signing anything.

- Be aware that traditional, reputable publishers won't ask you for any money towards the costs of producing your book.

- Be aware of vanity publishing – and know that vanity publishers don't refer to themselves in this manner.

- The job of promoting your book will fall on your shoulders if you are self-publishing. And even if traditionally published, you will be expected to do your share of promoting your book.

Exercise 1

Read up on what exactly vanity publishing is, so that you recognise it if you should come into contact with it.

Exercise 2

Are you feeling ready to begin writing your first novel?
Take it a step at a time and see how you get along.
Good luck!

Chapter Twenty-Three: Taking the self-publishing route

Step 1: Why self-publish?

The big difference between being published by a traditional publisher or self-publishing is in knowing that you're not alone in thinking you've written a good book. Someone else has endorsed that belief, and for a writer, that's a huge achievement and a boost to their confidence.

For many authors however, they choose to self-publish, not because they can't get a book deal but because they want full control over their book. For some self-published authors they will have already been traditionally published, but for one reason or another have come away feeling disgruntled about the process. Or they have their own reasons to self-publish a particular title.

If you choose to self-publish, then it might seem a daunting process. However, you don't have to go it alone. There is a lot of support, help and guidance on the internet and through books, magazines and workshops. A good place to start is The Alliance of Independent Authors. They are a professional membership organisation fostering ethics and excellence in self-publishing. They provide independent authors with trusted self-publishing advice, support, and resources. https://www.allianceindependentauthors.org/

Many writers these days choose to be independent authors for good reasons. For example, they may have written a collection of short stories or poetry, or their family history, or a non-fiction book on a topic that they are an expert on. Books which probably aren't going to find a traditional publisher. Or, as mentioned previously, because the author simply wants complete control over their book.

It's worth looking at the 'for and against' points before making a choice whether to go down the self-publishing route.

One of the big differences is that a traditional publisher will proof-read and edit your book, so that when it hits the shelves it will be as near word perfect as possible. The cover will be made, and the book will be distributed to bookshops and online outlets. It will also most likely, be produced in digital format as an ebook and available on digital platforms.

The publisher will probably have set in motion all kinds of marketing assistance and promotions to get news of your book out there. A big publisher has the money to put a lot of financial support behind your book. When you self-publish, you have to do all this yourself. Additionally, the author might have received an advance on sales from the publisher.

Reasons to self-publish

- You've written a personal memoir or collection of poems/stories that probably won't interest a traditional publisher.

- You love your book exactly as it is, and you don't want outside interference.

- You want complete control over your book.

- You retain 100% of the rights.

- You choose when to publish.

- You choose the cover design, the title and how your book looks.

- You retain the majority of the profits from sales.

- You set the price for your books throughout the world.

- You can keep a check on sales.

Reasons against self-publishing

- You can't be certain it's good enough to publish if only family and friends have told you it's good.

- You might be publishing a book that's not up to scratch and will get few sales and poor reviews.

- You can't get your book into the bookshops.

- You have to do all the marketing and promotion.

- You may have to pay out for editing and cover design.

- There's a lot of work to do in addition to the actual writing of the book and the costs are all falling on your shoulders.

Step 2: Prepare your manuscript for self-publishing

There are plenty of reasons to self-publish, but firstly, and obviously, you need to write your masterpiece. And you need to edit it as many times as necessary. Once it reads flawlessly and is as good as you can possibly make it, get some trusted readers (beta readers) to go through it and provide honest feedback. It is very difficult to be objective about a piece of work you've been slaving over for months, so a new pair of eyes should be able to give you honest feedback.

Your book must be grammatically correct. Writers don't always know they are making mistakes either in their writing or in their grammar. I would recommend you employ a reputable copy editor to go through your manuscript and ensure it is word perfect. Depending on whether you hope to produce paperbacks, ebooks or audio books, you'll need your manuscript saved in the relevant formats.

Step 3: Finding publishing platforms

So, your book is ready – but where to go with it? Time to research the market and find out who publishes independent books. You could approach a printing company who will provide you with an accurate quote for the number of books you're having printed. Or you could go to one of the online platforms, as listed below.

There are numerous print on demand and ebook companies which you will find by browsing the internet. Read their information thoroughly and work out precisely what the cost to you will be, and what exactly you get for your money.

Basically, the main cost comes from the initial setting up of your text in the correct format and appearance, along with creating artwork for the front and back covers and the spine. You might be providing these yourself, or you might need the company to provide them for you. Print on demand is exactly that, you can purchase as few or as many copies as you wish. The price to you as the author will be the price set by the company producing your books. You can set your retail price for customers to buy at whatever you like. Obviously, don't out-price yourself or you won't have many sales.

Every book has an ISBN number. This International Standard Book Number is a unique number by which any book can be identified, and be linked into the various marketing outlets where your book can be viewed, bought and sent out to the purchaser. Some companies such as KDP Amazon will provide the ISBN for your book. Or you can purchase your own. While you can just buy one ISBN, it works out more economically if you buy a set of ten. Contact: https://nielsenbook.co.uk/isbn-agency/

Don't miss out on the ebook market also. At the time of writing we are told that Kindle sales account for 82% of the English language ebook market. Amazon KDP is second in the list for self-publishing. And if you decide to publish your book exclusively to Amazon, you can enrol it in Kindle Unlimited. With Kindle Unlimited, you get paid by the number of pages read of your books. It's not a great royalty rate, but popular genres have tens of thousands of readers.

Whichever publishing platform you choose to go with, they each offer full instructions and guidance as to how to set up your books.

Here are some useful links to publishing platforms:

https://www.ingramspark.com/

https://kdp.amazon.com/

https://www.draft2digital.com/

https://www.smashwords.com/

https://www.kobo.com

Step 4: Selling your book

It's never too soon to start telling people about your book. Use social media, it's free. If you can start to drum up interest even before it's published, that will help sales. Whether you're an independent author or a traditional author, you have to become something of a marketing guru, finding ways and outlets to tell the world about your book.

Here's some ideas, I'm sure you will think of more:

- Look on the internet for free advice on marketing your book.

- Arrange a blog tour with book reviewers.

- Arrange a book launch at bookshops, libraries, community centres etc.

- Make yourself available to do talks on your book and writing career.

- Contact other writing groups.

- Get your book onto Apple, Book Bub. Good Reads, etc.

- Create an Author Central profile on Amazon – make sure it shows in as many different Amazon countries as possible.

- Build a website.

- Run a blog.

- Offer a newsletter.

- Create a mailing list.

- Offer your book free for a limited time to raise rankings.

- Ask people to write reviews for you. Be interactive with readers.

Exercise 1

Writers need an online presence. Consider building your website or starting a blog. If you already do these, consider creating a regular newsletter.

Important! Once your book is published, register for PLR, Public Lending Right. This allows authors to be fairly paid for every loan of their book from the library. **https://www.bl.uk/plr/applying-for-plr**

Chapter Twenty-Four:
Coping with Rejection

Step 1: What rejection does and doesn't mean

Every published writer will have had rejections at some time or other. Many great novelists have struggled to find a publisher for their masterpieces to begin with before going on to critical acclaim and to achieve best-selling status. So, don't let the fear of rejection put you off writing or make you afraid to send your work out.

If you get a rejection letter it doesn't mean that your work is no good or you're a failure. So, don't let it disappoint you too much. Books get rejected for all sorts of reasons. Possibly the publisher has recently accepted something similar, or perhaps it's too similar to something they've published in the past. Maybe it's just not to that particular editor's liking, whereas another editor might love it.

Be aware that rejection happens. Pre-warn yourself that you will handle it when it does – and that it will make you all the more determined to succeed. However, you can lessen the chances of rejection if your work is well written, that your presentation is excellent and you have sent it to an appropriate magazine or publisher. You can also increase your chances of success by having lots of work out looking for publishers at any one time.

Step 2: What to do with a rejected manuscript

When you receive a rejection letter, read it thoroughly, and if it offers any advice then take it to heart and learn from it. Take another look at your manuscript, see if improvements could be made and then send it winging its way to another appropriate publisher. Don't feel so downhearted that you put it away never to see the light of day again.

From my own personal experience, as mentioned earlier, I wrote seven different novels before getting the seventh one accepted. It certainly was a matter of perseverance and learning from my own mistakes. Once I started to get my books accepted, I could look back at rejected work and actually see why they weren't accepted. That enabled me to make the necessary changes and submit elsewhere.

I also learned that sometimes an editor would hint that the book almost made it but was rejected for a specific reason. If you get that kind of feedback, then act on it. Make the changes and let the editor know you've done so. Ask if they will take another read. After all, you've nothing to lose and everything to gain. On the occasions that I've done this, it's led to the books being accepted and published.

In a nutshell

- A rejection letter is just one editor's personal

opinion. Find another editor.

- Take note of any specific feedback you receive. If an editor has taken the trouble to point something out to you, it's worth taking another look at it.

- If there's an option to make changes and re-submit, then do so.

- If your manuscript keeps coming back, take a close read through and see if you can understand why. Ask trusted readers or writers for feedback as possibly it needs changes made.

Exercise 1

Browse the internet to discover famous authors who faced rejection. You'll be surprised!

Exercise 2

If you've had any rejections, take another look at what was actually said, and see if you can improve by re-working it. Then send it off to another publisher.

Chapter Twenty-Five: Beyond books

Step 1: Other writing opportunities

There is more to fiction than just writing short stories and books. Look at all the other genres of entertainment – TV, radio, stage plays, film, they all require writers. And they require a different approach, different techniques and different presentation.

You'll be pleased to know that here are courses, classes, workshops and books all packed full of advice from the relevant experts that go far deeper into each topic than I could do in this guide. My advice is to read as many 'how to' books as you can; look at the BBC website for guidance; look on the internet and in writing magazines to find courses and workshops. Immerse yourself in the particular genre that interests you.

Once you have the solid foundations and know-how for writing fiction and non-fiction, and your basic writing skills along with presentation techniques are second nature, there is nothing to stop you from progressing in any direction you wish.

Step 2: Writing for radio

There are some great 'how to' books available on writing for radio. However, for this book, I just want to touch on the subject, because getting your work broadcast on radio is a real possibility for a writer who wishes to take that route. There are radio plays, serials, short stories, talks and features regularly broadcast on radio. Find ones that appeal to you and listen to get a feel for them.

You will find radio at all levels: international, national, regional, community, hospital and college level. Radio is always going to be in need of good new material to broadcast on a daily basis. Tune in and listen to what is being broadcast and see where you could fit in.

Step 3: Writing for the BBC

The BBC Writers' Room is a must for anyone thinking about writing TV drama or comedy. The Writers' Room has news of opportunities, podcasts, competitions, how to submit a manuscript or pitch an idea and so much more. There's also a script library where you can download scripts of TV dramas and see precisely how a script should be presented. The website really is a wealth of information, and you can also follow on social media. https://www.bbc.co.uk/writersroom/

Step 4: Writing for the stage

As I have never had a West End stage play produced, I would not dream of trying to advise anyone on how to go about this. My own experience only goes so far as to have written, directed, produced and (occasionally) acted in six different pantomimes at my children's primary school some years ago. Certainly not big time, but a whole lot of fun.

The point is, there are opportunities out there to write plays to be performed by theatrical groups and Amateur Dramatic Societies. There are also competitions for plays of differing lengths. So, while you may not see your play on Broadway or the West End, it could very well be drawing in the crowds at your local Dramatic Society and being reviewed in your local newspaper; or winning a handsome prize in a competition. And from there – who knows? The stars, maybe!

There are books, information and advice on playwriting, plus workshops and courses. My advice to budding playwrights see as many stage plays as you can; familiarise yourself with play scripts, for content, stage direction and layout. See how actors and producers like to see the script presented. As always, give yourself the best possible chance to be up there in the running.

Step 5: Screenwriting

Writing for the big screen is very different from any other form of writing. And this book can only point out that there are many screenwriting courses available if you search online or in writing magazines. While some courses are free, many courses appear quite costly, so I would advise that you read reviews from people who have attended previously and decide whether you want to spend your money on such a course.

In a nutshell

- When you have the fundamental skills of writing under your belt, there is no limit to where you might go with your writing. The world is your oyster.

- Writing for radio, television, the stage or screen is a vast market with a voracious appetite for new stories. But it's a professional business, and you will only succeed in these genres when the basics of writing fiction are second nature to you.

- There are opportunities out there to learn the necessary skills, plus opportunities to write for these mediums.

Exercise 1
Download a published script from a TV drama that you have watched. Study how the writer provides the stage direction, as well as the dialogue.

Exercise 2
Whenever you have the opportunity of seeing a stage play, watch it with a view to learning from it (as well as enjoying). Analyse what goes on in the different scenes. See how the playwright handles time lapses and scene changes. Note also the special effects to see what is possible.

Chapter Twenty-six: The role of the literary agent

Step 1: Do you need a literary agent?

This is a question that every author ponders over. It's another of those chicken and egg quandaries. You can't get published because you don't have an agent and you can't get an agent because you aren't published. However, don't despair, there are agents who are looking for new talented writers. It's a matter of keeping in touch with what's going on in the literary world and submitting your work to possible agents when the opportunity arises.

But don't let the lack of an agent hold you back. While it's true that many of the big publishers will not consider unsolicited manuscripts and only look at work submitted by agents, there are still plenty of publishers who will look at manuscripts from un-agented writers.

Step 2: What do literary agents do?

Literary agents work with authors and publishers to get their clients' books published at the best possible terms. Authors do not pay their agents – the agent's fee comes when a publisher buys an author's work, then the agent gets their 10%, 15% or 20% (whatever has been agreed). You do not need a literary agent to get published. The benefit of having an agent is because publishers value their opinion, and know that if a manuscript has come via an established agent it will be to a certain standard and may be right for them.

Getting a literary agent is not easy. Agents earn their money through you, the author, so you need to be a 'viable proposition' for an agent to be willing to take you on. You can find a list of literary agents in *The Writers' & Artists' Yearbook*, and your first point of contact would be via an enquiry letter or email to see whether they would be interested in looking at your book with a view to representing you.

In a nutshell

- You don't need a literary agent to get published. But it often helps.

- The literary agent earns their money through getting the author the very best deals with publishers.

- A literary agent takes a percentage of the publishing deals they get for you.

- You don't pay a literary agent although some charge a reading fee.

- Publishers value the opinions of literary agents.

Exercise 1

Browse *The Writers' & Artists' Yearbook* and familiarise yourself with literary agents' requirements and what they are asking for. Investigate further through the agent's website or social media platforms.

Exercise 2

Write a review of this book for your favourite online book store, or email to me at: ann-evans@btconnect.com

Top tip

If there is one trait that a writer needs to develop on top of all their creative skills, it is PERSEVERANCE.

Useful links

The Society of Authors:
https://www.societyofauthors.org/

Public Lending Right:
https://www.plr.uk.com

Authors' Licencing and Collecting Society:
https://www.alcs.co.uk/

The Society for Editors and Proofreaders:
https://www.sfep.org.uk/

The Society of Women Writers & Journalists:
http://www.swwj.co.uk/

About the Author

Coventry-born writer, Ann Evans began writing as a hobby more than 30 years ago. It was a hobby that became a career and a way of life. She became a professional, multi-published, award-winning writer, learning the craft whilst bringing up her family.

After 'sneaking in the back door' of her local newspaper, *The Coventry Telegraph* as a grassroots reporter, she went on to become a staff feature writer there for 13 years.

To date she has published around 40 books, the genres being: children's and young adult fiction and non-fiction; reluctant reader books; adult crime/thriller, romance and non-fiction. She also writes short stories and has had around 2,000 magazine articles published on a wide range of topics such as: food, drink, gardening, animals, health, fitness, business, celebrities, antiques, collectors and more.

Her non-fiction writing really took off after teaming up with photographer Rob Tysall - Pro Photography. Together they are *Words and Images UK* and write regularly for a number of national and international magazines, print and digital magazines.

Writing has taken Ann all around the UK and to parts of Europe. Additionally, some of her books have been published in other languages including French, German, Norwegian, Swedish, Japanese and Thai.

Ann says: "My journey to becoming a successful, published writer has been through trial, error and perseverance over many years. But also, through the help, support and encouragement of family and friends, and some excellent editors and agents who I've been fortunate enough to work with.

"I love helping others who are keen to write and hope this Step-by-Step Guide will do just that. Thank you for buying it and please do leave a review."

Ann Evans

Books by Ann Evans

Non-fiction books
Become a Writer (Words & Images UK)
British Customs (Teach Yourself) (Brown Publishing)
Britain and the British (Brown Publishing)

Children's & YA books
Cry Danger (Scholastic)
Disaster Bay (Scholastic)
Deadly Hunter (Scholastic)
Fishing for Clues (Scholastic)
Stealing the Show (Scholastic)
Pushing his Luck (Scholastic)
Pointing the Finger (Words & Images UK)
The Beast (Usborne)
The Reawakening (Usborne)
Rampage (Usborne)
Children's History of Coventry (Hometown World)
The Trunk (Puffin Books)
Celeste (Clean Reads)
The Uninvited (Clean reads)
The Mysterious Indian Vanishing Trick (Fiction Express)
Warning Signs (Fiction Express)
Jump! (Fiction Express)

Picture Books
Lazy's First Christmas
Lazy at the Garden Centre
Lazy at the British Motor Museum
Lazy, King of the Castle

Reluctant Readers

Nightmare (Badger Learning)
Red Handed (Badger Learning)
Straw Men (Badger Learning)
Kicked into Touch (Badger Learning)
Spend Like a Celebrity (Badger Learning)
By My Side (Badger Learning)
Blank (Badger Learning)
Living the Lie (Badger Learning)
Keeper (Badger Learning)
Runaway (Badger Learning)
Promise Me (Badger Learning)
A Little Secret (Badger Learning)
The Prize (Badger Learning)
Message Alert (Badger Learning)
Viral (Badger Learning)

Romance
A Tropical Affair (DC Thomson/Magna Large Print)
Champagne Harvest (DC Thomson/Magna Large Print)
A Place to Belong (DC Thomson/Magna Large Print)
Highland Fling (Virgin)
Stowaway Bride (Solstice Publishing)

Thrillers
Kill or Die (Bloodhound Books)
The Bitter End (Bloodhound Books)

Featured in anthologies including:
13 Murder Mysteries (Scholastic).
Coventry Tales 1 & 2
Stories to Make you Smile
Authors Electric anthologies
New Shorts
The Coffee Break Collection
Telling Tales

Get in Touch

Website: http://www.annevansbooks.co.uk

Facebook: https://www.facebook.com/annevansbooks/

Twitter: https://twitter.com/annevansauthor

Instagram:
https://www.instagram.com/ann_and_rob_wordsandima
gesuk/

Linked In: https://www.linkedin.com/in/ann-evans-7211714a/

Blog: http://annsawriter.blogspot.com/

Blog: http://wordsandimagesuk.blogspot.com/

Index

Printed in Great Britain
by Amazon